Carolle Dupont

(450-   )

« The Traveller, the Wounded One,
And the Man with a Heart of Stone »

SKETCH BY MICAH TREMBLAY

Is there any prison greater than that of suffering?
Is there any heavier sorrow that binds?

To believe that every trial has a purpose
To discover, through this new awareness,
Other possibilities filled with hope
Which allow one to move forward
To confess in order to better understand
To receive because you have given
To season the past with forgiveness
These are the keys ...

May the message of this book move you
With the strength of its faith
With its honest desire to prevent
To help or to relieve
To rebuild, in brotherly love.

Lise Thibault,
Lieutenant-Governor of Quebec

Micah

Claude Tremblay

Micah

A father survives
the suicide of his son

ÉDITIONS JASPE

Translation : André Lefebvre

Graphics : Christine Lapointe
Document layout : Richard Leduc (www.multitexte.qc.ca)
Photos : Jacques Courtemanche, Pierre Langlois

Editing : Ken Gire, Lorraine Gray, Vivienne Galanis

Registration of copyright: Bibliothèque Nationale du Québec 2003
Registration of copyright: National Library of Canada 2003

IISBN 2 – 9805638 – 9 – 7

Printed in Canada

To my daughters,
Whom I love passionately

Annie
Émilie
Rébecca

FOREWORD

Losing a loved one... this can be the most arduous journey to travel.

The premature departure of my son leaves me with a scar that will never completely heal.

However, even in the midst of such circumstances, it is comforting to observe how the love of people around us can transform the most arid desert into the most fruitful garden. It is this kind of love that gave me the courage to write this book. I hope it becomes an oasis for many, where their strength is restored.

My sincere gratitude to all who encouraged and sustained me throughout the process of this literary project and beyond:

To my wife, Johanne, who has a heart as big as the world.

To my mother, and my brother and sisters, who believe in me.

To the whole team working with Jaspe: thanks for your help, wisdom, and listening ear ...at all times.

To the small group of people who meet on Tuesday nights: you are as dear as brothers and sisters to me.

To the ten doctors who wrote our previous book: your kindness has been of great comfort along the way.

A special thanks to Dr Luc Chaussé and to Lise. I will never forget what you did for me.

To my writer friend, Dominique Fournier, who has been there from the beginning of this journey.

Thanks to Jacques Noël. Your friendship is so precious.

Thanks to Evans and Donna for your hospitality during the writing of this book. I wanted to see the ocean...

Thanks to the school principals and teachers who took part in the subscription campaign.

Thanks to the Éditions de la Clairière for your help and patience.

I wish to highlight the good work of Jacques Charat-Boutique for distributing my books in Europe. It is a pleasure to work with you.

I also want to express my gratitude to Lorraine Gray, Vivienne Galanis and to Ken Gire who spent many hours editing my manuscript. Thanks for your love and your kindness.

Finally, and in particular, I want to thank all those who contributed financially to this project. Without your generosity, the publishing of this book would not have been possible.

CONTENTS

... *brain storm*

Your kind smile
Your gentle eyes
Your thousands of small bouquets
of daisies and dandelions
The fragrance of spring lilies
The Petzi stories
The "Amiral" pancakes
Your loving embraces...
Your little arms around my neck
The acrobatics in the living room
Your toys on the staircase
The "Happy Birthday, Daddy"
Your funny caricatures
Your drawings stuck to the fridge
Your drawings pinned on the walls
Your drawings displayed on our bedroom door
...your drawings carved in my heart
Your first bike
The kites...
Mario Bros 2
Your short prayers before going to bed
Your school bag left on the porch
Your toothbrush
The tree house in Repentigny
Skating on the ice rink
The sunny mornings
Your girlfriends calling
Your sisters teasing
The beauty of your heart
The marshmallows and campfires...
Ha! The campfires!
The games of "toc"
Playing shark in the swimming pool

16

Sliding in the snow
The avalanches in Hébertville
Brunette!
Your school marks...always very good
My failures
The promises with no future...
My unfairness and your wounds
My clumsiness...
The emptiness...
Summer vacations
The trips to Louisiana
Water-skiing at Lac-à-la-Croix
Grandma's yummy pies
Your school supplies
Your little shoes beside mine in the hall...
...Your big shoes beside mine
The puppets, "Pédro & Co."
Grandpa Broussard's doughnuts
Our rock collection
The sound of the skateboard on the pavement
The fights at school
The small pebbles at Campbellton
Fishing for mackerel in New Brunswick
Catching trout in Amqui
...I remember your first trout
...I remember your little hand in mine
...I remember the little bird feeder you built for me
...I remember your eyes, naive and true
...I remember...
...I miss you Micah
...I miss you so much
...I miss you so very much...

INTRODUCTION

Micah is gone! My beautiful Micah is not here! He is gone! Flown away! He's gone forever! And his presence …no one can replace his presence!

His departure blasted a hole in the dry soil of my heart. Deep… and wide… and dark. Like a crater…

And here I am, alone, at the bottom of my crater! Like an artist in anguish before his canvas. The storm is raging, black clouds rumbling. My brush races clumsily from the palette to the canvas. The wind blows with fury. The horizon disappears …my palette darkens! A shadow of light comes from nowhere, agonizing. My easel collapses... I give up! I lie down on the ground, my face in the dust.

The earth is still warm but trembles. I surrender! I can't fight this! The rain starts again, sudden, as a slap and just as painful. I keep silent until the anger subsides. Till a ray of sun wins out and in a flash pierces the thick armor of my wounds.

I am neither painter nor artist, but destiny has set before me an easel and a canvas. Although I feel powerless to face it, I am incapable of turning away.

Before leaving, Micah left me a picture, a sketch, a work I cannot hide under a pile of memories. It is a message he sent me… hard to penetrate because of its honesty.

From the pages of his notebook, a pencilled sketch opens a window to his soul, the soul of an artist, a wounded and anguished soul. This sketch, this cry from his heart, has become a sacred work. It moves me deeply. I can only look at it with reverence and respect.

For a long time I hesitated before taking up my pen to write this book about my son's death. To be honest, the idea did not originate with me, but rather, in a way, it came to me. It waited for me.

Shortly after Micah's death, my eyes lighted on this pencilled sketch, found among other drawings of his in a paper folder. My heart froze and I could not tear myself away from those three imaginary figures that seemed to know me so well. From that moment on, their shadow would remain with me forever. Whether I liked it or not, I had to face them. I knew that a painful but necessary dialogue had just opened up between those three men and myself.

It is not easy for a father to face his son's sufferings, and his own. Nor is it easy to express them openly to others. But I will do it, for Micah, and for me. Hoping the emotion my son tried to communicate through his drawing will bear fruit in my life as well as in the lives of other fathers and their sons who, I wish with all my heart, will never have to face the struggle that was ours. I also think about those mothers, brothers, sisters, friends, and family members also shaken by such a loss. May this story help you crest the jagged peaks of sadness, and glimpse the sprawling vistas of peace.

⤜⤛

This drawing from Micah calls unto me, troubles me.

A wounded man, young, exhausted and suffering, facing the first moments of death. Wounded… my son?

A strong muscular man, a traveller, carrying this poor wounded soul in need of help, on his back.

An emaciated character, insensitive, authoritarian, morbid, sitting in the sand, petrified by indifference. Did Micah draw this man with the heart of stone, thinking of me?

The Wounded One

Neither god, nor man...
Peaks too high, roads too long...
Rather dark horizon...
I am falling
Dark and gray sky
My scratched CD
Of Kurt Cobain in Nirvana,
The pain tears my heart out
The sinking sands of silence
The angel's dance
"Riding on the storm"...
My head hurts
I pray all would stop
No answer comes
The hill is slippery
I scream, I yell,
Alone in the crowd
Prisoner in society
I walk beside my shoes
I'm letting myself go
I'm letting myself go...

C.T.

FAREWELL MICAH!

THE DAY OF MY BIRTH was a celebration. Nine months of preparation; everything was beautiful. Snuggled in my little habitat, gently, soothingly rocked in my parents' love, impatient as they were to see me, kiss me, and give me the greatest treasure on earth... a happy home.

Opening the door, I saw the light and cried for joy, and cold hands tore me away from my mother's arms as she was getting a shot of narcotics... then silence.

Happily, all was quickly forgotten...

My parents understood all my cries: the cry of hunger, the cry of joy, of fear, or of hurt. Silence was very soft at the time. Tucked in and warm, at my mother's breast, I listened to her heartbeat. And, like a ticking sound, like a familiar melody, the whisper of her voice rocked me: "Tonight, my soul longs for tenderness."

There is plenty of love at home, many moments of celebration, much joy, many toys, candies, tropical fish, a dog, and a little white mouse. I cry with delight, I laugh, I sing, I dance.

Silence is my friend. At times he comes to caress my cheek, to run his hands through my hair as I am busy colouring or looking at picture books. He comes closer to me in summer as I lay down in the tall grass to look at the big, fluffy clouds on their way to the land of dreams.

Silence plays with me. Sometimes he blows on the leaves, makes ripples in the river; he carries the scent of strawberries, wild flowers, and evergreen trees in his hand.

But the years passed, and the silence changed. My parents changed, too. And our home changed. Our happy squeals of delight have become sounds of strife and contention, war. And I fear being hurt. I shared my sadness with the silence but too often this friend betrayed me. So I hid in my room. But the silence followed me, locking itself up with me.

My room has become my fortress. Darker tones cover the walls. Childhood dreams are fading. The white mouse is getting old, pacing back and forth in its cage. I don't cry anymore, I am angry. I don't question any more… I seek other methods of expression. Plugged into my CD, listening to heavy metal music, I learn to speak "trash", "death". My soul cries, searching. My dream falls into a cave …my dream …my nightmare.

I am like a mute carp falling into the depths. And the deeper I descend, the darker it becomes. Everything is closing in on me. The silence is oppressive. I can't even hear my own heartbeat. I am dying. And my relationships are dying with me.

My girlfriend has found someone else, and I remain alone, silent.

Like the wind, and just as lost …just as listless.

-⫸✦⫷-

One day, I reached for my sketchbook and surrendered to whatever my fingers wanted to draw. It turned out to be a sailboat! Magnificent! With a high, straight mast it glides on the water, bent to the will of the wind, free as a bird. It's a beautiful day. The orange sun warmly caresses the blue sea. This is a great boat I have drawn here! I love sailboats. I like to look at pictures of them in books. Like the nice boats Vincent Van Gogh painted.

I like Vincent. He and I understand each other.

24

Once he painted four little boats on the shore. Waiting on the white sand, they tell stories of dreams and adventures at sea. One has a name: Friendship. They are impatiently waiting for the sailor to haul them to the salt waters to join their friends already bathing, their sails puffed by the wind.

How I would have loved to meet Vincent, become his friend, his apprentice! See life with the same eyes and express it with the same passion! I would have loved to travel, discover the world and return to my friends to tell of my adventures, to share my discoveries with them!

One day Vincent told his friend, Bernard: "I finally saw the Mediterranean Sea, which, most probably, you will cross before me. I spent a week at Saintes-Maries, and to get there I took a stagecoach and crossed the region of Camargue with its vineyards, meadows, and flatlands, just like in Holland. There, in Saintes-Maries, some girls reminded me of Cimabue and Giotto — thin, straight, a little sad, and mystical. On the flat, sandy shore, I saw little green boats, red, and blue, so nicely chiseled and with such colors, they remind one of flowers."

How I would have loved to be there with him! To take in the whole of the sea for the first time! Breathe in the salty wind! Hear the cry of the white birds!

Tell me, Vincent, what has the sea told you? And those girls, how did they make you feel? Say, Vincent, you also drew sketches when you were sad and lonely, didn't you? Yes, of course! You could depict the boats as little flowers, to be picked and given to all the lonely people across the centuries. So they too could dream a little.

-≫×≪-

I look at the beautiful sailboat that Micah has drawn, and it makes me dream of happy days long gone.

From birth, Micah displayed the traits of a gentle, affectionate, and generous person. He wasn't the gloomy type, but rather active and teasing. Other people were important to him.

He would often give up his rights to keep harmony in a group or to bless someone.

Living in peace mattered a lot to him. So did having fun. Whether sketching on his pad or playing with friends, Micah's tender heart revealed itself. This tenderness of heart invited some abuse from his peers. He usually knew how to avoid it, but at times, undeserved harshness, mockery, and haughtiness hurt him deeply.

His tolerance threshold remained particularly high and, as a general rule, he was quick to forgive and to work at rebuilding relationships. So much so that large numbers of children loved to hang around in our backyard or basement.

A river flowed close to our house, and on hot summer days we often would go there to swim together. I smile at the memory …the outbursts of laughter from Micah, his three sisters, and their friends. We would walk in the river, arm in arm, bucking the current. At times, we would struggle to keep our footing and not be carried along by the strong waters or the bubbling rapids. Nothing really dangerous! During the long winter months, we would go to the municipal pool and each time was quite a party. Do all children do this? In our family, four little kids would find great joy constantly climbing back on the springboard to carry out the most daring and goofy jumps, but only when they had the undivided attention of one, or both of their parents. For them, that attention made all the difference. And each time I was delighted to congratulate them. Micah's small, skinny and brownish silhouette easily stood out from the line-up at the board, waiting his turn. From time to time, I would teasingly look away just to hear him eagerly yell "Papa! Watch me jump!"

On warm Spring days, we enjoyed going to the forest, on foot or by bike, to watch the birds or simply have a family picnic. A mile or so from the house, there was a lake where we would often go to watch the great herons and catch frogs in the swamp. And after putting off heading home thousands of times, wanting still more time to play on the swings at the park, we would slowly walk home amidst the chatter of Micah and his sisters, arguing about who would get the best

26

seat in the little cart, or who would carry the binoculars around their neck.

Autumn brings such pleasure to children in Quebec, right after the apple season, gathering huge amounts of dried multi-colored leaves and spending hours rolling and wrestling on these thick, cushy piles. I remember being totally buried under a mountain of leaves by eight laborious and playful little hands. I can still smell the fragrance of those dried leaves and hear the voices of Micah and the girls giggling and saying, "Let's bury papa under the leaves!"

I remember another moment (Micah must have been seven or eight at the time) when we bought a kite. It was a sunny day, we went to a big park by the St-Lawrence River where I taught him how to tame and maneuver this bird. Marvelling at the sight, he was clutching the string with his tiny hands and looking at the sky where our fragile "mono-plane" was high and flapping away. Suddenly, the wind got nasty for a second and the string snapped. Here we were, all silent. Micah, his mother, the girls and I just stood there, watching the kite twirling away among the clouds.

We went back home, deeply saddened.

⊰≫×≪⊱

The most precious treasures are not necessarily the most expensive ones.

The city of Amqui, where we lived for many years, was only two hours from the ocean. To us, a visit to the ocean was a holiday. We loved sprinting in the sand and then in the waves, amidst splashes that danced in the sunlight like sparkling diamonds. For hours we would walk along the shore, looking for small, coloured rocks to add to the family treasure. Actually, I don't remember ever leaving the beach without carrying a load of little rocks and shells of all shapes and sizes. Then, in each of the children's shoes and in their jean pockets, was all that fine sand that would end up on the bathroom tiles or on the bedroom carpets that night.

I still savor those moments. Micah, the eldest, swift and agile, always ran ahead to make sure he had first pick of all the rocks and pebbles of the beach. He would quickly fill up his two pockets, and with hands full, would run to me or to his mother to share his discoveries. He would fold them in a beach towel and then return to his laborious prospecting. Annie, a little younger than Micah, would sometimes succeed in convincing him to take her as his treasure-hunting partner. As for the two youngest ones, Émilie and Rébecca, they longed to emulate their older siblings and would grab any rock or common shell as an excuse, and bring them to the "cache". Always careful, however, never to mix them up with those their brother and Annie were collecting. I would never tire of walking with my children and enjoying the simple pleasures of the ocean. It brought me back to my own childhood, and to me those multicoloured rocks, shells, and fragments were real treasures, treasures that no amount of money could buy.

As the years passed, I lost many of those rocks, but I did managed to keep quite a few of them. They nestle in a straw basket on a shelf in my office. They represent a touching memory of the deepest kind. Now, whenever I go back to the seashore alone and pick up a little coloured pebble, when I look at it in the palm of my hand, something seems to break in my heart.

Many little rocks were lost over time and many dreams broken in my life and in the life of my son. How did we get here? I don't know! Rather, I do know, but would prefer not to think about it. I would prefer to go back and start all over again. I would like to be given another chance.

I didn't always keep my promises and Micah shut the doors. My expectations were unfair at times, and he closed his mind. Unwittingly, I betrayed his confidence and he turned his back on me for good. I am left with remorse, memories and confusion.

Wounds and suffering without forgiveness leave me with dreams of days gone by.

-≫×≪-

But the wounded one, in Micah's sketch, can't dream anymore. He has no strength. His wild eyes are protruding, terror blurring everything they see. Even the blue sky has turned gray. He doesn't see the beauty of the little boats, the golden sand, and the turquoise ocean waves. He does not hear their soft whisper gently rocking his soul. He hurts. His shaved head, stripped of its beauty, can no longer contain the rushing waters of his random, often incoherent thoughts.

He trudges through this nameless desert. The smallest dune has become an impassable mountain. The once friendly sun tortures him. He is weary. His lips are parched. He tries to call for help, but he groans. Sinking sands are swallowing him up …he won't make it out!

He is thirsty but there is no water. Only mirages, and empty hopes. He loses all faith.

I think about the distress of this agonizing one, and I hate myself for not having been able to help my own son.

I don't know where to turn in order to get rid of my shame. Any explanation from others seems empty and any compassion from others seems undeserved. I wish that the whole universe would be my judge and condemn me so I could serve my sentence and be freed from this unbearable guilt.

I wasn't able to understand my own child. I can hardly stand myself. I can hardly look in the mirror or hear my name spoken.

I would like to redeem myself, but Micah is not here anymore. I look for him everywhere, digging deep into the memories, but even my thoughts play tricks on me, betraying me. If only I could have a fresh start, we would sit together and I would listen to him for hours. But he is gone!

Often, I need to be alone, to get away, so I can look back into the past and understand where I have failed. I realize my failure to discern Micah's sensitive emotions, and I spiral down into an abyss of regret.

When I try to find relief in sleep, I wake up abruptly. I would like to cry, but tears have deserted me. I wish I were dead!

--->><<<--

Surely Providence places a sign on our path, an indicator to help us through the desert of our lives. True, we don't always see it clearly, but nevertheless, certain events do occur along the way to guide us.

I work as the director of a small publishing house, and one of my tasks consists of acquiring translation rights to American best-sellers and publishing them in French to distribute in French-speaking countries.

One day, my attention was drawn to a book written by Ken Gire: *Windows of the Soul*. It attracted me first by its beautiful presentation: the magnificent landscape on the cover, the red fonts at the beginning of each chapter, and the well thought-out layout. However, what got me to read and later translate it, was the table of contents, which revealed the book's emphasis on poetry and the arts. Gire explains how art has always been an essential element in society and how some very talented artists have been rejected because of the misunderstanding of insensitive people of their era. He teaches us to understand the artist's soul, opening their daily lives to us so we can share in their passions and struggles.

This book was a road sign, to show me that other artists, like Micah, were deeply hurting. The sudden departure of some of them also left parents, friends, and relatives grieving and confused.

One of the stories, about the painter Van Gogh, left a permanent impression on me. After reading it, I reacted the same way Ken Gire did a few years earlier. I went to search for the three huge volumes of letters that Vincent wrote his friends and family during his lifetime, and I became entirely engrossed in them. Reading them broke the silence about the taboo subject of suicide. A dialogue was opened for me about a theme I would previously have left untouched.

I grew to love Van Gogh and appreciate the incredible beauty of his soul. And despite the tragic ending of his life, he is the one who opened my eyes to things I was unaware of in my own life. Although I wished that neither Vincent, nor Micah, nor anyone else for that matter, would leave this world in such a desperate way, I wanted to be able to receive as their legacy the treasures they wanted to give me.

I discovered through Ken Gire's book that the very young Van Gogh wanted "to sow the words of the Bible" amongst the poor of the working class. Preparing for that task, he would sit at his desk every night copying words from the Bible, page by page, translating them into English, German, and French. "I read it daily", he wrote, "but I should like to know it by heart and to view life in the light of its words." In London, he went to the city slums to preach to the poorest of the poor. Sensing a call to follow in his father's steps, he studied theology. However, Vincent's temperament, his zeal and eccentricity, kept religious institutions from embracing him. A fellow student remarked that "he didn't know the meaning of submission." Maybe that would explain why the authorities of the Bible College gave him a "concession" rather than a "commission" to be a "lay evangelist" among coal miners in a small town.

The miners lived in horrible conditions. They suffocated in the dark womb of the earth, poisoned by methane vapors, which also threatened to explode. Added to that was the threat of underground water seepage, which caused the old tunnels to collapse. Working excessively long hours broke their backs. "Most of the miners", commented Van Gogh, "are thin and pale from fever. They look tired and emaciated; weather-beaten and aged before their time."

On September 24, 1880, he wrote his brother Theo: "The miners and weavers still constitute a race apart from other laborers and artisans, and I feel a great sympathy for them."

Vincent Van Gogh lived with these people and shared in their poverty. He went down into the mines to be closer to them, breathing the same toxic, dusty air. He visited their sick, bandaging their wounds and praying with them. And on

Sundays, he preached to them, trying to communicate some ray of hope, some spark of encouragement for their coal-darkened lives.

"I should be very happy if some day I could draw them", he said to Theo, "so that those unknown or little-known types, would be brought before the eyes of the people."

And he did so.

The German poet, Rilke, later wrote that this period was the beginning of Van Gogh's artistic life, "and so he became what is called an evangelist, going to a mining district and telling the people the story of the Gospel. And while he talked, he began to draw. And finally he didn't even realize that he had stopped talking and was only drawing."

Van Gogh's extreme altruism, his zeal, and his resolve to oppose the status quo bothered the ecclesiastical authorities and he was fired. He left the pastorate, angry and bitter.

At the age of 27, Van Gogh entered another episode of his short stay on earth: he became an artist. "I want you to understand clearly my concept of art," he wrote Theo at the beginning of that journey. "I want to do drawings which touch some people. Whether in figure or landscape, I should wish to express not sentimental melancholy, but a serious sorrow. I want to progress so far that people will say of my work, 'he feels deeply, he feels tenderly'."

Van Gogh was fond of workers, the poor, and particularly the oppressed. He painted a peasant busy sewing clothes, women working in the soil, and farmers having a meal after a long hard day in the fields. Another of his paintings shows two kneeling women praying, a baby on its mother's knees, and a young girl fondly watching over a baby in a crib.

"In a picture, I want to say something comforting, as music is comforting. I want to paint men and women with that something of the eternal which the halo used to symbolize…"

His sketch, *At Eternity's Gate*, shows an old man sitting on a chair, his face buried in his hands. "What I have tried to portray in this drawing," said Van Gogh, "is the inexplicable emotion emanating from the image of an old man, sitting motionless in his corner by the fire. What seems to me one of the strongest proofs of the existence of God and eternity, speaks of something precious and noble which cannot simply be destined for worms."

Strangely, nobody seemed to understand what this artist was trying to express. He spoke a language that was difficult to understand. Through the years, rejection, solitude, and depression finally prevail over his sanity. His spiritual health declines as well. The gradual erosion of his faith is revealed in the letters he wrote during the decade of his career as an artist. We notice that references to the Scriptures and God, as well as the musings about his faith, gradually vanish as his anguish and despair progress. His night was getting darker and his confusion was increasing.

On May 8, 1889, Van Gogh, hurting, was admitted to the Saint-Rémy-de-Provence asylum, a few miles from Arles, France. He was given a small, sparsely furnished room.

In the meticulously researched movie about Van Gogh's life, *Lust for life*, we see Vincent shown to his room by a nun who, once inside, offers to open the window. He nods for her to go ahead. Then he looks outside and gazes at the fields fading in the distance, bathing in the sunlight. This moment is a turning point for him. His little room now a studio, he starts to paint again.

His window overlooked a garden where flowers bloomed. They inspired his first painting in this asylum. In the lower right corner of the picture, he simply signed "Vincent" and titled it simply *Irises*. This painting was the beginning of his return to health.

Van Gogh stayed at the asylum, and his health improved for a time. It is during that same year that he finished *Starry Night*, where we discover the darkness of Vincent's soul, but also the stars. "This raises again the eternal question: Is the whole of life visible to us, or do we in fact know only the one hemisphere before we die?" For my part I know nothing with certainty, but the sight of the stars makes me dream, in the same simple way as I dream about the black dots representing towns and villages on a map".

Theo still perceived this light in Vincent's soul, but all the others could see was darkness, and for some time now, no one even cared to look.

"There may be a great fire in our soul, yet no one ever comes to warm himself at it, and the passers-by view only a wisp of smoke rising from the chimney, and continue along their way," wrote Van Gogh.

How sad was his life; that rich sensitivity, those fears, those emotions shared so passionately. And the people kept their distance, shaking their heads as they walked away. Gradually, Vincent's physical, mental, emotional and spiritual life collapsed. It was night.

Only Theo understood the passion filling Vincent's heart, this fire burning, burning, until finally consuming him. The painting, believed to be the last spark to set the canvas ablaze, was done in July of 1890, and titled simply *Cornfield with Crows*. Vincent wrote to Theo concerning this work: "A vast field of wheat under troubled skies, and I did not need to go out of my way to express sadness and extreme loneliness."

It is in one of those fields that Vincent ended his life. The bullet lodged near this heart. The wound wasn't immediately fatal, and he was taken to his room, where people quickly sent for a doctor. His brother came to be with him. The following day, on July 29, 1890, at one-thirty in the morning, as Theo was holding him in his arms, the artist uttered his last words: "La tristesse durera". *The sadness will never go away.*

-->><<--

Last night I didn't sleep well. I was agitated and had a horrible nightmare: a young man roughly nineteen, Micah's age, made a deep cut in his chest, through which I can see his heart beating. There is no blood, but this is one of those dreams where all is dark and gray, where there is no color. In fact the darkest spot is precisely this gaping gash in his chest: an obscure crevasse, a black hole. I am losing it. I run around in confusion, pushing the injured young man on a stretcher. Terror grips me as I see his face contorted with the intensity of the pain and the fear. I try desperately to find help by any and all means, but without success. I get lost in unending mazes and hospital corridors, never able to find a doctor.

Upon waking up, I am weighed down by indescribable sadness. This emotion leads me to the hospital room in Sherbrooke where I witnessed the agony and death of my son. This sadness causes me such pain!

I know we've arrived at the point, in the telling of this story, where I have to relate the dark hour of Micah's suicide, and I'm scared. It hurts so much. And it seems the sadness will never go away.

If only I could have done something to prevent this tragedy! How long has he really thought about taking his life? Why didn't I succeed in restoring our relationship? Why couldn't he forgive me? Was his anger blinding him to the truth in my eyes? Why do so many parents, brothers, and sisters, have to endure this terrible suffering and live with this heavy sadness in their soul? When will these tragedies end? Will the sadness ever go away?

-≫≪-

It was a hot summer night. At six o'clock in the morning, the police find Micah kneeling on the street. He is completely disoriented. What he says makes no sense, and he seems to be hallucinating, pointing to the sidewalk and the street. He is not aggressive. An ambulance with a police escort takes him to a hospital where he is admitted, completely delirious. He is evidently suffering from a drug overdose, as empty pill bottles are found in his bag. During the day, Micah remains agitated and incoherent. The Quebec Center for Poison Control is called to inquire about the effects of certain substances, which he seems to have ingested. He is admitted to Intensive Care where he is treated for his symptoms.

Around midnight, the hallucinations stopped. Micah utters his first coherent sentence and says he's doing better. He is helpful and calm. During the night, he becomes agitated again. His temperature rises. Around six-thirty a.m., as blood is taken for testing, Micah rips the tube from his arm. They administer Haldol, a powerful sedative.

Twenty-four hours after his arrival, new tests are done. These reveal that the intoxication was a mix of substances. He is transferred to another hospital where they are already making the preparations to hook him up to a dialysis machine. However, as soon as the tubes are inserted, Micah dies. All resuscitation efforts fail.

In more technical terms, the coroner's report adds the following details:

"During Micah Tremblay's hospitalization, various factors contributed to the maintenance of a course of action based on the first temporary diagnosis, rather than questioning the diagnosis in view of the patient's evolution and the emergence of signs and symptoms indicating primary intoxication with salicylates. These symptoms (tachycardia, hyperthermia, and diaphoresis associated with alkaline respiratory metabolic acidosis, alkaline pH) all pointed toward salicylate intoxication. Micah Tremblay displayed all of these symptoms.

Because the salicylate poisoning was immediately dealt with, no other control tests were performed during the day or the night before his death. They were considering the possibility of Gravol poisoning instead. (This substance was not found in Micah's personal belongings or during the toxicology screening.) And during the night the resident doctor did not think it necessary to investigate the cause of the hyperthermia. The problem was that the intoxication was caused by a combination of drugs, and this factor was not suspected.

Micah Tremblay had therefore initially absorbed an undetermined quantity of salicylates and diphenhydmates. Post mortem toxicology tests clearly demonstrate that the amount was toxic.

However, the true reasons leading the victim to commit this act remain unknown."

The Traveller

To whom does one turn
When the source of tears runs dry?
To whom can one turn
When death seems sweeter than life?
When the soul cannot find a way
Out of the abyss
When sighing is all one can do,
When the source of tears runs dry?
To whom can one turn
When we cause but grief,
To those around us?
To whom can one turn
When our tears weary our friends?
When the world offers no comfort,
When there is nothing left to try?
When the source of tears runs dry?
To whom can one turn?
To whom can one turn?

CHRISTIAN HYMN

THREE LITTLE PEARLS

THE MAN WITH A HEART OF STONE remains impassive. He does not speak, frozen by his indifference. The wounded one is also silent and weak. The traveller suddenly finds himself between two poles: total indifference and extreme agony. And he, the sensitive one, is preoccupied with the wounded one's anguish and disconcerted by the coldness of the man with the turban.

Aware of the critical state of the wounded one, the traveller tries to resuscitate him, to comfort him. Placing a hand under his head, he gives him a drink, softly caressing his fevered brow. But time is short, and he doesn't have what it takes to heal him. Lifting the man onto his shoulders he struggles along, hoping to find help. Periodically he changes the position of the wounded one, carrying him sometimes on his back and sometimes like an infant, in his arms.

His steps get heavier. One last time he reaches for his flask, only to find it empty. His knees give out; his ankles no longer support him. Desperately dragging himself over the sand with his heavy burden ... he does not give up.

-»><«-

I know a great truth about friendship: "A true friend loves always, and in adversity becomes a brother." It is correct to say that there are seasons in life when only the tenderness of a friend can calm the raging storm. At other times, even the presence of those we love cannot soothe the violent winds and tides which threaten to engulf our souls. How hard it is then for a friend to share in the suffering. He feels totally helpless. And he is pained to see a loved one succumb to his sufferings, unable to have comforted him.

I think of those who must face the sudden, crushing reality that a part of them has been snuffed out, the silver cord broken. Perhaps a spouse, a parent, a brother or sister, a son or a daughter, a friend, sometimes one's doctor, social worker, teacher …all people who, at one point in their lives, took someone else's burden upon themselves, hoping to help. Under a scorching sun they carried a companion or an exhausted friend who was too tired to go on. Crushed under the weight of another's sufferings, they found themselves crawling in the burning sand, searching for help.

My thoughts turn specifically to three young women I deeply love who witnessed their brother's life slipping away. They watched helplessly. Each one of them, together with their brother, had woven a unique tapestry, bright with thousands of embroidered, colored threads. And even if this work of art, this precious fabric, was a little less brilliant in certain areas, the colors were in soft harmony with the overall pattern of their young lives. But now a thread has broken, a thread of unique color, irreplaceable, one that will change that artwork forever. It's as if suddenly, strangely, all the colors in the tapestry have darkened.

Partly because of her age, Annie, the eldest of my three girls, was very close to Micah. She was even a bit of a confidante. Gentle and loving. Always seeking to understand others. She probably carried her brother's burdens many times, just as he would surely have done for her. Discreet and respectful, Annie is easy to confide in. You can trust her with secrets and not fear she'll betray you. She and Micah spent many long hours together. They probably shared their problems; problems common to all young people, …their dreams, their extravagances, but also their deceptions and frustrations.

I saved a letter Micah wrote to his sister, which she wanted to share with me after he had gone. Written with simple words, words of kindness, with a touch of humor as always, affectionate feelings sometimes mixed with worries and sadness.

It was as if the young adult in him suddenly awoke, looking around and rubbing his eyes, hoping life was only a dream, hoping that the tumultuous night of adolescence had only been the fruit of his fertile imagination. Hoping that some memories could vanish like shadows fading into the sun at dawn.

He wanted to forget those nightmares, looming in shades of black and gray, where you run aimlessly, out of breath, never going or getting anywhere. He wanted to forget those dreams where people we love fade into endless nothingness; to forget those haunting fears that hold us back from the challenges and mountains we feel are too great; to forget those nights of love and ecstasy that, in the morning, strangle and choke us like a thick fog. He wanted to forget those sometimes impulsive twists in the road of his youth. Micah would have preferred to avoid them.

But here, thousands of miles away from home, sitting with a warm cup of coffee, he is no more the carefree teenager, but rather the young man, writing home. Spontaneously reaching for a piece of paper, he tenderly pens a few words of advice to his sister, hoping she will avoid those sufferings and disappointments. He wants to warn her about abuse of all kinds, about sharks lurking, and the slippery road of easy love. He wished to tell her of the dangers of alcohol and drugs. He wanted to tell her about the ill-fated consequences of his own mistakes, hoping his honesty would help her on her own journey.

Annie shared this moving letter with me, which Micah had sent her when he was in New Orleans. For almost a year he lived there with his grandparents, working with them in their small bakery.

My children really loved Louisiana, their mother's birthplace, and we often traveled there together. For us, these occasions were always a celebration. And for the grandparents, what a joy to be able to kiss and hug their little penguins.

As a young adult, Micah might have chosen to go back there to earn some money and experience new things. Was he looking for a place of refuge where he would feel good about himself, a peaceful harbour where he could better understand who he was? Was he looking into the African-American culture to discover his own roots? Or did he unconsciously want to copy his parents, who had, at his age, crossed the Americas in their journey into the "peace and love" culture? Maybe all of these were fragments of the mosaic of his being. But hundreds of miles from home, his family, his mother, and his sisters occupied his thoughts. He was reflecting on life, on things he had done. He expressed his affection for his sister whom he loved so much. He also expressed his worries.

Shortly after his return to Quebec, he found a job in a bakery in Sherbrooke where he made new friends. Then he joined a *death metal* band as a guitar player. Their music was nothing other than an act of vomiting against society and against God. Micah christened his guitar "Excalibur". He dived into a thick darkness where he took part in the occult and satanic rituals. That proved fatal!

After a series of conflicts at home, he finally settled downtown. He got his own apartment in one of the worst parts of the city, infested with all kinds of perversions, drugs, and alcohol. And this is where he decided to end his life.

The door was still ajar, empty beer bottles scattered across the floor, a glass bowl half filled with liquid paper, empty sleeping pill containers, and, on the bed, Excalibur, with a short note to a friend stuck between the guitar strings, bequeathing the instrument to him.

After Micah's death, I found a poem written by Annie. My heart broke as I read it. I felt her pain. I felt her tears.

Gray clouds
Cold nights
Sad and alone
Such is my life.

Winter
When all is dead
When the cold abides until dawn
When the freezing hail
Reaches and pierces my heart.

Winter
Dark and dreary
When icicles pierce my shadow.
When the hills, slippery and steep
Cause me to despair
And render me helpless.

The clouds, the nights
The cold, the gloom
The sadness, ... lonely
Such is my life.

How can I comfort her?

I try, in my clumsy way, to be a friend to each of my girls. For a long time now, I have given up the image of the hero-dad with all the answers. All I know is that I love them dearly and feel true sadness when I hear the heavy sighs coming from broken hearts.

Annie and I sometimes go to a restaurant during the summer months. We share interesting ideas about life, our opinions about movies we have seen, the talent of actors whose names I never can remember. On one of those occasions, we went to hear Bruce Cockburn play, and later that night, we talked about Micah's death. It is always difficult for us to talk about it, and we cried together. I have come to understand there is a time for everything, and there are sentiments that should not be forced. I must respect the time each healing requires, but it is hard to see those tears well up in my beloved daughter's eyes and feel totally powerless to ease her sorrow.

On that particular night, however, I believe God must have seen my distress, for through one of Bruce Cockburn's songs, he comforted and reassured me. He showed me the way. He simply told me to love.

Heavy northern autumn sky
Mist on forest
Dark spruce, bright maple
And the great lake rolling forever
To the narrow gray beach.

I look west along the red road of the frail sun
To where it hovers between the shelf of cloud
And spiky trees, receding shore.

The world is full of seasons
Of anguish, of laughter
And it comes to mind to write you this:

Nothing is sure
Nothing is pure
And no matter who we think we are
Everyone gets his chance to be
Nothing.

Love's supposed to heal
But it breaks my heart
To feel the pain in your voice.
But you know
It's all going somewhere...
And I would crush my heart
And throw it in the street
If I could pay for your choice.

Isn't that what friends are for?
Isn't that what friends are for?

We're the insect life of paradise
We crawl across leaf or among
Towering blades of grass
Glimpse only sometimes the amazing
Breadth of heaven.

You are as loved as you were
Before the strangeness swept through our bodies,
Our houses, our streets...
When we could speak without codes
And light swirled around like
Wind-blown petals at our feet.

I've been scraping little shavings
Off my ration of light
And I've formed it into a ball
And each time I pack a bit more onto it
And I make a bowl of my hands
And I scoop it from its secret cache
Under a loose board in the floor
And I blow across it and I send it to you
Against those moments when the darkness
Blows under your door.

Isn't that what friends are for?
Isn't that what friends are for?
Isn't that what friends are for?

And that's what I want to be for my children. A true friend. With my imperfections, my failures, my illusions ...yet a true friend. One who will never give up, despite the circumstances. That's what God taught me, and that's what I'll do. Believe in love.

Émilie and Rébecca also suffer from the loss of their brother. In the hospital room where death had just passed, I could still see them, frozen, powerless, their eyes filled with sadness and fears. Again, near the coffin, confused, hesitant, frail, and unable to surrender to such fate. Rébecca later found the words to describe this distress:

Love,
It appears,
And flows down a cheek.

Tears.
Black and white was all I thought.

45

When a good friend dies…
It's just like being a prisoner

When love breaks apart,
Your heart does the same.

This terrible tragedy was and still is, difficult to overcome. A part of ourselves was ripped from us and the mend-
ing is very slow. This unwelcome rupture is hurting us. We
have to learn to live and overcome this feeling of anguish by
taking care of one another.

We enjoy going to the movies together. Certain movies are
like a balm to our wounds. I gave in to tears when in *CastAway*,
Tom Hanks, after surviving four years on a deserted island,
watches his dreams shatter again, as he must leave the one he
loves forever. I cried watching the ending of *Armageddon*
where Bruce Willis says goodbye to his daughter through a
computer screen thousands of miles from earth …moving
scenes speaking to us about the painful separations we all must
face.

Watching *Finding Forester,* with Sean Connery in the
lead role, I identified with this old writer who was both
grumpy and endearing. I felt his loneliness and the heaviness
brought about by years of living. I greatly enjoyed the young
black man from The Bronx, and the relationship that slowly
developed between those two characters. Through this movie,
I learned that true friendship conquers the barriers of culture
and age. I learned that friendship leads to forgiveness. And
that friendship lasts forever.

The road is long for me to become a better friend for my
daughters and those I love, but I know I'm walking in the
right direction.

After our nights at the movies, we sometimes share our
comments, and sometimes we remain silent. However, the ice
cream parlour is a sacred stop, a chance to pause and share
more than a late-night treat. We don't always succeed in
expressing the love we feel for one another, but with a smile,
a tender touch or look and, coming from Émilie, a sponta-
neous comment or joke, we know our hearts are one. Without

words, we believe that the difficult trial of Micah's departure will make us into more sensitive and stronger people. And with God's help, today's pain might one day become a healing balm for others.

These few verses written by Émilie to her sister Annie may best express how they have grown from the hurt caused by the loss of their brother. Such acts of love between my daughters are like rays of light piercing through the thick dark clouds of longing.

Dear Annie,

The clock of his life has stopped
His time has ceased
While mine keeps on going.

Time goes on, time is crying,
How does one stop grieving?
His time has now passed
Leaving my heart to collapse.

In my memories, his time is engraved
As I cry my good-byes, my time goes on.

P.S. I love you, Nini. Don't let time hurt you.

How important are those well chosen words and little notes my daughters use to communicate their sadness and their love. In so doing, they encourage each other. I see them sometimes lying on the couch watching TV, and without realizing it, they come closer to one another like purring kittens. They are happy to be together ...and in those moments, I am happy too.

I am proud to be the father of these three beautiful girls, and I pray constantly that their future will hold true happiness for them. I pray that the men they marry will be affectionate and caring, that they will be men who love God and love life.

I sometimes smile thinking of days gone by. I smile at the picture of Émilie looking at me with her bright little eyes when she succeeded for the first time in keeping her balance on her bicycle without the training wheels. I can still see her darting in front of her two sisters, wanting to be first in all the games. She was so eager to win at the game of Toc, for example, that we had to watch her constantly so she wouldn't cheat. She made us laugh a good deal... our little dynamo.

Thinking of Annie makes me smile also as I remember that magnificent day when we decided to go for a long bike ride. I can see her beautiful brown hair blowing in the wind, her smile, and again I sense the happiness of that moment. The sky quickly darkened and we were in for an incredible shower. We quickened the pace, laughing, but got completely drenched anyway. The sun came back out as fast as it had disappeared.

I think of my little Rébecca, whom I often took for a piggyback ride on my shoulders. Her gentleness and the little notes she wrote me, words of encouragement with beautiful drawings. I have preserved them as precious treasures.

I see Rébecca taking pictures of Émilie and me as we fed the horses on the ranch where I lived. We were giving them small wild apples, which we found in the forest, and they loved them!

I am happy to have lived so many great moments with my children. I'm blessed to still be able to be with them, in spite of the circumstances. I believe in them and am convinced their courage will allow them to succeed in the life they choose.

I love them dearly and trust that I have been able to pass on good values to them and make them understand that happiness is often found in little acts of love and in small things.

Faith gives us the courage
to face the uncertainties of the future.
It will give our tired feet
new strength as we continue
our forward stride toward the city of freedom.
When our days become dreary
with low-hovering clouds
and our nights become darker
than a thousand midnights,
we will know that we are living
in the creative turmoil
of a genuine civilization struggling to be born.

MARTIN LUTHER KING
Nobel Prize Acceptance Speech

REMEMBERING LOUISIANA

IT WAS IN 1972, IN NEW ORLEANS, that I met my children's mother. I was seventeen and she was fifteen. At that time it was the custom to drop out of school and hit the road in search of adventure. When I was only sixteen years old, I had taken a first trip to Spain and Morocco, and the following year I spent six months in California and in the south of Mexico before heading west to the city of New Orleans, in Louisiana.

My new girlfriend's parents, Herman Broussard and Barbara Duet, lived in a small impoverished district close to downtown. All the residents were black, as was half of the population of New Orleans. I remember this little white house with the dark green skylights, set on cement blocks like so many other houses in the south because of the terrain and the humidity.

Along the hill by the house, a few vegetables grew. One of them was this strange looking plant that produced little green cones about 3 inches long; it was called *okra*. If it is not prepared properly, this vegetable becomes slimy, but Barbara created gourmet dishes tempting enough to get me to indulge in a bowl of *okra gumbo* more than once, with a big piece of warm thickly buttered cornbread on the side. What a feast! And behind the house was a tall pecan tree that gave the most delicious pecans. You can take my word for it: nothing compares to Louisiana pecan pies!

At that time, Barbara worked as a secretary and Herman as a baker and real estate agent. Later, Herman bought his own little bakery, and it has become a family business.

I first saw the girl I was to marry in a park around the Vieux Carré. She had just decided to leave town and go to California without telling her parents, but she changed her plans and decided to come with me instead. Two days later, we were on our way to Canada. This sudden and unannounced departure created quite a stir and brought extreme anguish to the Broussards. Herman and Barbara were convinced that their oldest daughter was dead. It was to be five months before we got in touch with them. They were sad and broken-hearted.

Happily, our relationship with them improved over time. Then, one beautiful day in December, dressed in sandals and Indian cottons, we got married. We lived in Canada and were rarely able to visit the grandparents, but when we did, those visits were all the more precious. The children reveled in Grandpa's delicious, plentiful doughnuts. I believe the year Micah spent in Louisiana with his grandparents was a great one for him and I wished he could have stayed longer. The time spent with his grandparents was beneficial, and working with his grandpa did him a lot of good.

Soon after his return, Micah showed signs of positive change. For one thing, he was more comfortable with giving and receiving affection. Even the way he dressed was tidier. Herman shared with me that on a few occasions Micah went to church with him, of his own accord.

Herman and Barbara are engaging people, and a happy couple. The long years of sharing life have woven strong bonds of love between them that no trial has been able to break. However life hasn't always been easy for them. Raising a family in a black district of New Orleans is a challenge. Despite poverty, high crime rates, and racism, they courageously stayed the course, diligent in their work and they instilled good values in their children.

I must also mention that they lost their older son, Herman Jr., who from a young age, suffered from rheumatic fever. The illness damaged his heart and an operation was necessary. As he became an adult, his health deteriorated, causing new heart problems that were fatal. It was a tragedy for the parents and the whole family.

Before marrying their daughter, I lived for almost a year with the Broussard family. I was the only white man in that district, but I was accepted by the black community and considered by the vast majority as one of them. Not only did I discover the richness of the Afro-American culture, but also the Creole and Cajun cultures. I became friends with young black men and I was happy to see the racial barriers fall, as well as the resentment imposed by centuries of injustice and oppression.

Herman, Barbara, and their five children, are mulatto, but they have skin that is almost white. In the south of the United States even if you have a small percentage of African blood, you're considered a Negro, and that's what they put on your birth certificate. Their native tongue was French. Barbara's great grandfather came directly from France by boat to find the acadian Louisiana of his parents. Mixed marriages had already created a new ethnicity that they named "Creole", a mixture of Acadian, Spanish, and African races. Barbara grew up in the region of Pointe-à-la-Hache. At that time the region was populated with many Creoles, Blacks, and Cajuns. Her father was a carpenter and her mother stayed home to care for their eight children.

Her uncles grew vegetables and oranges that they sold in town at the market in the French quarter. Other members of the family, like Uncle Lionel, hunted in the bayous in the shadows of the great oaks, gathering oysters and shrimp for market.

As a young girl, Barbara liked to tag along with her uncles. She remembers the big alligators suddenly appearing out of nowhere, swimming beside their little boat. "They did not scare me," she claims, laughing, as she recalls her childhood, "but I believe that if I went back today, I wouldn't be so brave."

Here is a woman not lacking in courage. A few years ago, Barbara had a brush with death. She was mugged. A black man was hiding in the Broussard's van that was sitting in the parking lot of a supermarket. As she started the vehicle, he hit her several times on the head with the butt of his rifle before throwing her on the pavement. She was so disfigured that it was almost impossible for her husband to recognize her at the hospital. She suffered serious wounds and numerous contusions. The consequences were unavoidable, but thanks to the prayers of her family and the members of her church, she miraculously recovered. There is no psychological or physiological sign of that terrible ordeal. She even told her story on American television.

In spite of this terrible experience, Barbara did not lose her good nature or her faith in God. She is an exceptional grandmother.

Herman's childhood was less privileged than that of his wife. He was born in another part of Louisiana, in Youngville, near Saint Martinville, home of the Cajuns. At that time, the only language spoken in that region was French, a brand of colorful French with expressions unique to the Cajuns. Herman was born after the divorce of his parents and never knew his father.

At the time, the white population considered the blacks of the southern United States, especially those of Louisiana and Mississippi, inferior. Though slavery had been abolished, blacks were given only second rate jobs, working in sugar cane plantations and cotton fields. In public areas, signs reading "Whites Only" were always present near water fountains, and the train stations were divided into sections for "Whites" and "Blacks". The same principle was applied in the city buses where a chain-link fence separated the seats allotted to whites and blacks, the latter, of course, located at the back of the bus. Even in church, the best seats were reserved for the white people.

Such circumstances weren't easy for Herman's mother who had to work hard just to survive. Herman was forced to live with his grandfather, Oscar Raymond, and later on his great uncle's farm. At the age of nine, he got his first job with a truck driver, delivering huge blocks of ice destined for the iceboxes of the villagers. At the time they did not have electric refrigerators.

When he was twelve years of age, Herman worked in a sugar refinery. After a short stay in a boarding school, he was sent home to live with his mother in New Orleans. He was fifteen. This is where, for the first time, he got a job as a baker, a trade he practiced all his life. After buying his first bakery, *Sunny's Bakery*, he made the local headlines with his famous *"King's Cake,"* a traditional cake of the Mardi Gras festivities.

His fondest childhood memories take him back to his birthplace with his brother and his friends, spending hot summer days swimming in the *Taché* bayou, one of the rare bayous unvisited by alligators! And today, he is enjoying a happy retirement with his cherished Barbara and he never tires of sharing the goodness and faithfulness God has shown him throughout his life. I am happy that, despite the circumstances that caused the break-up of my family, we have remained great friends.

I will always remember our visits to Pointe-à-la-Hache. I met many uncles, aunts and cousins who spoke fluent French. Uncle Lionel and Uncle Joe always told their hunting and fishing stories with great pride while Aunt Rita, in her kitchen, prepared delicious dishes (*gumbo* and *jambalaya*) in great quantities. I can still smell the spicy aroma of the cooked crab and giant shrimp that Uncle Lionel caught, and I can still see all those people enjoying themselves around the table in sheer simplicity. I also remember a couple who was so old that the wife couldn't even remember how old she was, cousins René and Nicie, from Saint Martinville. They only spoke to each other in French, and I suspect they even had a hard time communicating in English.

I always felt at home with those people. I liked their honesty and good humor. I will never forget this period of my life nor the magnificent Louisiana landscape. These pictures create the most beautiful backdrop to my memories: huge moss-covered oaks, looking like old men; the gardens on the banks of Pontchartrain Lake; the giant palm trees along Gentilly Boulevard; artists displaying their works near the park at the heart of the French Quarter; the big doughnuts cooked in oil at *Café du Monde*; and the old jazz musicians of *Preservation Hall*.

I can still hear the crickets' song at sunset that is characteristic of hot and humid climates. I can still see the little black kids with their big, bright eyes playing in the street at night before their parents rounded them up for bedtime. I think of gentle Miss Marie, whose grandmother had worked as a slave in the cotton fields. I remember exuberant Kim, our cousin, and the stories Uncle Curt told with passion. I feel nostalgic when I think of the family meals with Kerwin, Darren and Lisa – all precious people I was privileged to know.

I know that all of these people suffered with us when they heard of Micah's death, and the bonds of love between us have been a source of great comfort during this trial.

-»>«-

Days go by and memories remain, but sometimes it feels as if they are playing hide-and-seek. In the weeks following Micah's death, I experienced incredible memory lapses. Often as I lay on the bed, I reached for the memories to come and comfort me. But so often I came up empty-handed ...as if I had been robbed of those images from my past, like words on a chalkboard that had been erased. Those memories had flown away with my son's soul, replaced by an oppressive nothingness, a horrible fear of never recovering, the fear of spiraling into despair to the point of having to be admitted to a mental institution. I could not, in those moments, shed even one tear. And I was ashamed of that.

Gradually rediscovering the pages of my life has been reassuring. But there are still days when grief takes over and I become orphaned from my memories and any joy they might bring. The problem is that I am unable to face this painful reality: never again on this earth will I see Micah. And this is precisely what disturbs me and hurts me.

What is there to do?

Do I engage in long weeks of work even if I don't have the strength? Roam the bars every night for entertainment to dull the pain? Meet people who don't understand me? Kill time in front of the TV all night long? Escape through sleep or stay in my room, isolated and brooding over dark thoughts? What misery! When will this whirlwind finally let up?

I realize that I must go on living one day at a time. But I'm running out of solutions.

I am not superstitious, and I do not believe in the powers of fate, as some would call it. But I do believe in hanging onto God and trusting him despite these overwhelming feelings of depression. God never promised that everything would be easy down here, but he did promise that he would always be with us and would guide our steps. And that is enough. At least for me.

Last summer I made a decision to take a vacation where I spent a few sunny days near the Bay of Fundy on the coast of Nova Scotia. It did me a lot of good. But on returning to my office, I couldn't stop thinking about the small seaside village of Baxter's Harbour that I had just left. I was well aware of the "blues" that vacationers experience when they go back to work after spending two magnificent weeks of rest by the sea. However, this was not the type of nostalgia that I was feeling. I loved my work and I was happy to get back into it, typing on the computer keyboard. This time, though, it was as if I had to put all my other editing projects on a shelf and focus on something more urgent. I had an irresistible desire to pack up my bags and leave for a meeting I could not afford to miss.

I know this will seem absurd, but that's what I did. I left, bringing my notes and manuscript with me, and I settled in a little cabin near the ocean at Baxter's Harbour, that was without telephone or computer. As soon my mind was made up, a deep peace came over me... and I was convinced I had made the right decision.

Very early one morning, I went to the sea, to a remote place that was hidden between the rocks. I took with me some fresh fruit in a bag as well as the red folder that contained the text of the book that I had begun to write. I picked up my pen and let the words flow from where I had left off a few weeks ago ...and my memories reemerged.

I had never really stopped to consider the history of Louisiana and the Broussard family. Though I knew, of course, that the Cajuns had been deported, I didn't know anything about the time and circumstances in which these events occurred. Most of all, I was ignorant of the fact that Nova Scotia, this land which was now under my feet, had been populated by the forefathers of my children. I came to this region to be close to the sea, to its rocky shores, to its high tides …and to take advantage of the peace and quiet I needed to face with my memories.

I knew almost nothing of the real story of this beautiful and humble people known as the Acadians …until I found myself at the historic site of Grand-Pré, near the Minas Basin and the Bay of Fundy, only a few minutes from Baxter's Harbour.

Here I was to learn a lot about the epic journey of the Acadians.

The war was over and the spirit was broken
The hills were smokin' as the men withdrew
We stood on the cliffs
Oh, and watched the ships
Slowly sinking to their rendez-vous
They signed a treaty
And our homes were taken
Loved ones forsaken
They didn't give a damn
Try'n' to raise a family
End up the enemy
Over what went down
On the plains of Abraham
Acadian driftwood
Gypsy tail wind
They call my home the land of snow
Canadian cold front movin' in
What a way to ride
Oh, what a way to go

THE BAND
(Album: Northern Lights - Southern Cross)

GRAND-PRÉ

IN 1524, AN ITALIAN EXPLORER by the name of Verrazano used the name "Arcadia" to describe an area he was exploring along the Atlantic coast of North America. He was inspired by a poem written in praise of a place in ancient Greece known for its pastoral beauty. Later on, in maps of the New World, the name had evolved to Acadie, and designated an area now known as Nova Scotia, New Brunswick, and part of Quebec and Maine. Some say the name Acadie came from the *Mi'kmaq suffix e'kati*, meaning, "land of" or "place of."

The region was first inhabited by the Wabanaki people (later called Abenaquis by the French), one of the migrating tribes of the eastern forests. This tribe was made up of the Mi'kmaqs and the Malecites.

During the seventeenth century, a colony of 500 French settlers established themselves in Acadie.

The children of these settlers can be considered the first Acadians, and today they number a few million people.

Pierre Melanson, also called La Verdure, along with his wife, Mary Mius d'Entremont, and their five children, were the first to settle in Grand-Pré, around 1680. They wanted to distance themselves from Port Royal, the colony's capital, where they were often the target of attacks.

Melanson and the settlers who came to join him later knew that the soil around the shores of Minas Basin was suitable for farming. With limited means (forks, shovels, cattle,

61

and horses), they erected dikes (called aboiteaux) and transformed the fertile marshland into useful soil for agriculture and for pastures for their cattle. The people of Grand-Pré and the surrounding region became the largest of the Acadian communities that settled along the Bay of Fundy and Nova Scotia coastline. Soon the entire colony was sustained by produce from the Minas region. The Acadians of Grand-Pré led a peaceful and prosperous life.

Their common origin, their very strong family and religious ties, and their deep love for the land developed in them a strong spirit of solidarity over time. They were politically neutral. Even though they occupied a territory of strategic importance for France and Great Britain, who were disputing between them the supremacy of North America, the Acadians refused to take sides in the conflict.

In 1730, as the war was raging, they were pressed by Governor Phillips to signed an oath of conditional allegiance which, they were led to believe, would ensure their neutrality in an eventual conflict. But this neutrality clause was only a verbal promise and the ambiguity of this agreement contained the seed of a tragedy.

In 1755, when the conflict between the British and the French intensified, the British authorities decided to deport from Nova Scotia those they referred to as "the neutral French." Acadian members of parliament, gathering in Halifax to present a petition, were imprisoned. On August 19, 1755, Lieutenant Colonel John Winslow arrived at Grand-Pré with his troops. Saint Charles Church became his headquarters, and on September 5, the men and boys of the Minas region received an order to gather at the church where Winslow read the order of deportation.

"Gentlemen, — I have received from his Excellency,
Governor Lawrence, the King's Commission which I have in
my hand, and by whose orders you are conveyed together, to
Manifest to you His Majesty's final resolution to the French
inhabitants of this his Province of Nova Scotia, who for
almost half a century have had more Indulgence Granted
them than any of his Subjects in any part of his Dominions.

*What use you have made of them you yourself Best Know."
"The Part of Duty I am now upon is what thoh Necessary is
Very Disagreeable to my natural make and temper, as I Know
it Must be Grievous to you who are of the Same Speciea."
"But it is not my business to annimadvert, but to obey Such
orders as I receive, and therefore without Hesitation Shall
Deliver you his Majesty's orders and Instructions, Vis:"
"That your Land & Tennements, Cattle of all Kinds and
Livestocks of all Sorts are forfeited to the Crown with all
other your effects Savings your money and Household Goods,
and you yourselves to be removed form this Province."*

Grand-Pré, September 5, 1755

The order of deportation was enforced by a troop of
2,000 volunteers from New England, joined by 250 British
soldiers stationed in Nova Scotia. More than 7,000 men,
women, and children were transported by boat to the colonies
along the American Atlantic coast. To dissuade the Acadians
from returning to their land, their villages were burned. Their
houses, barns, windmills, and all the other buildings were
reduced to ashes, leaving little sign of the Acadians who had
lived there for more than a century. A great majority of the
deported never saw their native Acadie again.

The exile to British colonies was even crueler than the
deportation was to these people. Dispersed into small groups
within the towns and villages, they lived among a population
extremely hostile to their presence. A law passed at the
Massachusetts legislature illustrates their living conditions
well. It was decreed that if the former French inhabitants of
Nova Scotia were found beyond the borders of the districts
the government established for them, they would be subject-
ed to ten lashes of a whip on their bare backs.

Governor Lawrence had recommended that the young
Acadian children be removed from their families in order to
turn them into good English subjects. Many followed his
recommendations to the letter and didn't hesitate to use force
to remove even the very young children from their mothers.

Further to the south, in Virginia, the deportees were turned away and sent to England where they remained in concentration camps in Bristol, Liverpool, South Hampton and Portsmouth. More than half of those exiled died of sorrow, deprivation, or were victims of contagion. The shipwreck of two boats also cost the lives of many other Acadians.

The deportation officially ended in 1764, but the migration of Acadians looking for a homeland continued for another fifty years.

In order to acquaint myself better with this tragic episode of history, I went to Saint Charles Church in Grand-Pré, which has since been restored and is currently a museum. My heart was torn as I read the original, handwritten text of the order of deportation, from the pages of Winslow's journal.

What misery! What injustice toward such a peaceable people! My eyes met with one of the frescoes painted on the walls of the church. It illustrated the harvest: women, with long dresses and white aprons; men, rakes in hand, joyfully toiling to form grass bundles near the "aboiteaux" on the banks of the Minas Basin; a young girl holding a jar of cold water or cider and pouring a glass for her fiancé.

Then, a scene of the deportation: men, women, children, and sad, confused old folks waiting on the shore; couples embracing and hugging each other one last time; an old man with his arm around the shoulders of a little girl, while a small puppy pulls at the hem of her dress to invite her to play. Here, a British soldier, in a red tunic, is escorting the settlers. There, four women with their white bonnets, motionless and silent. Another woman holding a child in her arms, watching the rowboats as they move towards the English ships. Her husband is in one of them …she will never see him again. What a sad outcome for those poor people!

A wide glass cubicle in the center of the museum displays ancient artifacts, objects discovered through archaeological digs. There were fragments of clay dishes, the bottom of a bottle made of French glass, pieces of porcelain painted with small blue flowers, a brass faucet from a wooden barrel, buttons from a jacket, a brass thimble, part of a clay pipe, French coins and English money, and an old jew's harp. All of these artifacts from another age came to life before me. I imagined this old Acadian playing his jew's harp, surrounded by young people dancing energetically on the wooden floor.

I see pretty little gabled houses, ...and it's mealtime. The mother proudly sets a steaming casserole on the large table, surrounded by a multitude of children laughing and teasing, while the fathers look on, smiling. I inhale the fragrance of the freshly cut grass, mingled with the smell of the salt air blowing in from the basin, and carried to the village by a gentle breeze. In the shadow of an oak, a grandmother watches a small child, with hair gold as wheat, bouncing around with a little cat, as her skilled fingers push a needle through silk. I see young people with glowing eyes, sitting by the sea, on a Sunday afternoon...

Suddenly, I am jarred back to reality by a group of boisterous tourists from New York who enter the little church of Saint Charles. Back to earth, I continue my visit.

I see another hall, a smaller one, in the back, with charts depicting the journey traveled by the Acadians as they searched for a new homeland. A little farther on, a small, framed picture captures my attention. I come closer. I am suddenly overwhelmed with emotion by what I see! Here is a copy of the original text of an appeal that one Acadian deportee wrote to an English governor. What a sad picture! Here is a man, a wanderer in one of the New England states, pleading for the lives of himself and his family:

"To His Excellency Sir Thomas Pownal, Captain General and Governor in His Majesty's Province of the Bay of Massachusetts in New-England Honoured Counsel and House of Representatives.

The Petition Francis Meuse (Mius) humble presents.

"The petition of Francois Muise humbly sheweth that your petitioner formerly an inhabitant of Cap Sables in Nova

65

*Scotia, a part of that country always friendly to ye English,
and ready particularly to relieve the Fishermen, who
frequently experienced their Protection and Hospitality,
was placed, after he was brought to New England, at Salem
with his Family, being twelve persons in all, where he abode
9 months and by the favour of the People and their own
works, were comfortably subsisted.*

*But that after 9 months, The Government thought fit to
remove them to a Town called Twesbury, where they suffered
much, it being a small poor Town, very little work to be found,
and for the little they do there is hardly any Pay to be got,
so that though they are able and willing to work, they lose
the Advantage.*

*They are lodged in the most miserable house in the world, all
the timber rotten, not one square of glass in the house, no
chimney but a few stones pil'd up to the height of about six
feet, and then a hole open thro the top so that they are smoked
to Death; add to this, that at every blast of wind they expect
the House to be down upon their Heads, and think it a
miracle that it has stood so long.*

*Your Petitioner prays your Excellency and Honour to
consider the miserable condition he must be in during the
Winter in such a Situation, and to order him some Relief,
He prays particularly that your Excellency and honours
would be pleased to remand him to Salem from whence he
was removed where he lived comfortably and inoffensively
and where He and his Family can find the Means of support-
ing themselves by their Labor & industry, with little expence
to the public.*

And your Petitioner shall ever pray. "

*Francis X (his cross) Meuse
Boston, January 6, 1759*

For a while, I remained silent before that text. "And your
Petitioner shall ever pray". It was echoing through all the halls
of my spirit. "And your Petitioner shall ever pray" …Isn't that

what I should be doing for all the people who, like this poor Acadian, live in the deepest of distress!

There are many other things I could do to lighten the burden of the suffering, but isn't prayer also an important thing to do? It was the least I could do, to kneel and ask God to give needed strength to that one who is breaking under the burden of his trials —as He gave strength to the Acadian people to overcome their struggles and sorrows.

I was about to leave the little chapel when I noticed a large metal plaque engraved with many inscriptions. I drew closer, not suspecting that I was about to discover a historical reality that would transform my relationship with the Acadian people and directly involve the lives of my own children.

On these plaques were engraved the names of all the Acadian families who had lived in Grand-Pré. Intrigued, I perused the list: Meunier, Olivier, Pellerin, Poirier, Préjean (known as Le Breton), Richard (known as Sansoucy), Richard (known as Cadet), Richard (known as Boutin), Samson, Terriot, Thibodeau, Voyer, Le Blanc (many of whom, afterwards, had to change their names to White), Dupuis (who became Wells), Le Jeune (Young), Gosselin, Guérin, Hamel, Landry, La Vigne, and suddenly Broussard…BROUSSARD! The name of the mother of my children! Incredible!

Unknowingly, I was walking on land that had been cultivated long ago by the ancestors of my own children! I had to investigate further.

Make me a bed of fond memories
Make me to lie down with a smile
Everything that rises afterward falls
But all that dies has first to live.

As longing becomes love
As night turns to day
Everything changes
Joy will find a way.

BRUCE COCKBURN
(Album: Joy Will Find A Way)

BEAUSOLEIL-BROUSSARD

AMONG THE ACADIANS living in the region of Miramichi during "Le Grand Dérangement" (the deportation), Joseph Broussard, (also known as Beausoleil) was one of those who distinguished his generation. Born in 1702 in Rivière Port Royal, a village of ancient Acadie, he was the son of François Broussard and Catherine Richard. In the mid-eighteenth century, over a period of about twenty years when French and English fought in Acadie, this man made his mark in the Resistance. In fact the English perceived him as one of the leaders of the Acadian Resistance.

It was around 1749, after the founding of Halifax that the tensions between France and Great Britain increased again. The tensions escalated to open conflict, resulting, among other things, in the conquest of Fort Beauséjour in 1755, and the beginning of the Acadian's dispersion. During those tumultuous years, Joseph Broussard was called to play an important role as an Acadian soldier. He was allied with the Indians, among whom he enjoyed a good reputation, living among them and speaking their language. Father LeLoutre, a missionary priest from France who played an important role in the history of the Acadians, had a great esteem for Joseph Broussard and his brother Alexandre. Besides being independent fur traders, the Broussard brothers brought reports on the activities of the English troops to Father LeLoutre. When, in May of 1755, the English besieged Fort

Beauséjour, the Broussard brothers hurried to the Fort and took part in the battle. A French officer praised the merits of Joseph Broussard and said that he was, among the Acadian fighters, one of the bravest and most determined. Following the exhortations of Father LeLoutre, he and a group of Acadians and Indians, succeeded in capturing an English officer. Broussard fought to the end, and on June 6, the day of Fort Beausejour's surrender, he led an attack.

He accepted the defeat reluctantly. Two days after the surrender, he came to see the commander of the British army, Lieutenant Colonel Robert Monckton, and acted as a mediator between the English officer and the Indians. He agreed to negotiate peace, on condition of his own amnesty. Monckton consented to the pardon on condition that Broussard receive the assent from Lieutenant Governor Lawrence. We are led to believe that this assent was never granted, because a few weeks later, Joseph Broussard along with many Acadian patriots fell into a trap set by Commander Monckton. Soon afterwards, he was deported to South Carolina.

In February 1756, Broussard escaped and rejoined his wife and children in his beloved Acadie. Accompanied by a few Acadians, he reached the Mississippi River and then Quebec in the middle of the summer. He rejoined his family at the mouth of the Petcoudiac River. Encouraged by the French authorities, he once again became a leader in the Acadian Resistance. Governor Vaudreuil, encouraged by the Acadians, allowed him to arm a small ship navigating in the French Bay (Fundy) and organize attacks against the English troops that were now at Fort Beauséjour and Fort Port-Royal. The village of Beausoleil became one of the main training camps for the Acadian Resistance.

On July 1, 1758, a contingent of English troops inflicted a severe blow to the Acadian patriots at Petcoudiac. During the battle, Joseph Broussard was wounded. History reports he also lost a son in the exchange. The wounded Broussard went to Miramichi for medical care at the same time the English took the fortress of Louisbourg. The conquest of Louisbourg positioned the English strategically and they were now more able to attack the Acadian refugee camps where the main leaders of the Resistance were staying. That's how in mid-September 1758, they attacked the settlements located at the mouth of the Miramichi river, where Broussard was allegedly in hiding. They burned houses and churches but took few prisoners, all the inhabitants having escaped further inland. Two months later, in mid-November, the villages on the Petcoudiac river, among them that of the Broussards, were pillaged and destroyed. At the same time Broussard's ship was seized, along with a boat which the Resistance had taken from the English. This meant the end of the Resistance of the Acadians of Petcoudiac since in November 1759, the Acadian Resistance of Petcoudiac, as well as those of the rivers Miramichi, Richibouctou and Bouctouche gathered at Fort Beauséjour to sign a surrender.

Despite their promise to meet at Fort Beauséjour in the spring of 1760, many Acadians preferred to stay underground. Joseph Broussard and his son were among them. They had taken refuge in the region of Miramichi, more precisely at the mouth of the Burnt Church River, a place far from the English troops stationed at Fort Beauséjour.

It is at Restigouche, during the summer of 1760, that the last battle of the Seven Years War occurred. Even though the English came out victorious, Broussard and his men were not disheartened: a month after the battle, we find them again at the Saint-Jean river where they continue their attempts to intimidate the English. It seems, however, that their actions were in vain, for during the winter of 1761, the commander of the French troops at Miramichi post, Grandpré of Civerville, surrendered arms, thus complying with the terms of the surrender of Quebec. Broussard, still at Miramichi, headed a small group of Acadians who desired to pursue the Resistance.

In the summer of 1761, Pierre du Calvet, former store manager for the Crown at the Miramichi post, made a list of all the Acadians living on the coast, from the Gaspésie to the Miramichi River. Joseph Broussard and his family were still in Miramichi and the English suspected that he was one of the main instigators of the Acadians' refusal to surrender. General Amherst then ordered the commander of Beauséjour, Captain Roderick Mackenzie, to go and drive out these last Acadian rebels. Upon arriving in Miramichi, Mackenzie and his men could not arrest Broussard who, having heard of their plan, found refuge in the forest. In the report produced for his commander, Captain Mackenzie noted that the main leaders of the Acadian Resistance had been apprehended, with the exception of Broussard. Here is what he wrote:

"This fellow I believe may be Catch'd this Winter or Spring by Scout snow shoes which I will be ready to try if you think him worthy So much notice."

It probably happened this way, for, in the summer of 1760 we find Joseph Broussard and his family prisoners at Fort Edward in Pisiguit.

In the beginning of the year 1763, peace was signed between France and England, thus putting an end to the Seven Years War.

Many Acadians, wishing to live in French territories, refused to swear allegiance to the British Crown. In November 1764, many of them prepared ships in Halifax and sailed for the French West Indies. Broussard's departure is noted as occurring during the last week of November. His goal was to reach Saint-Domingue, and from there he would travel to the state of Mississippi. They succeeded, and in the spring of 1765, we find Joseph Broussard and his family in Louisiana. On April 8th of the same year, the commander of this French colony named him Captain of the Militia and Commander of the Acadians of the Attackapas region. Broussard didn't occupy this function for very long as he died on October 20th. He was sixty-three years old. He was buried "at the camp called BeauSoleil", a site located near Saint-Martinville and the city of Broussard. To this day, Joseph Broussard (also known as Beausoleil) is considered a national hero in Louisiana.

It is difficult to describe the deep impression this saga of Acadian history and particularly Joseph Broussard, had on me. I feel a deep respect as I read the stories of those courageous settlers. I feel that a part of their character is found in my son and daughters.

Peering through those painful pages of history, I gain an understanding of my own grief. I also draw strength from the courage of those people. Their stories help me to dig deeper past the roots of my own life to the roots of Micah's, where I might discover the causes of our successes and our failures!

What I have no trouble picturing is the pleasure I would have felt if Micah had been at my side to explore the treasures of our past, exchanging our comments and our feelings, wondering together at the discovery of the Broussard's family ancestors. What would he have thought of Joseph Broussard? Without nurturing resentment for the English, I can but admire the courage of that man, his perseverance to fight for a just cause, and his incredible tenacity, even in the face of defeat. Would Micah have shared this admiration? Would he have understood the deep commitment of this courageous fighter to defend the weak? Would he have recognized his affection for the Indians, an affection that drew him to live among them and learn their language? Would Micah have felt this passion, this strength that flowed in Broussard's veins, this devotion to his homeland? I think so. I think Broussard's thirst for justice resided in the heart of my son. His commitment to others, his love for the weak, the little ones, — I often witnessed them in his life. This great passion that allows us to climb the highest mountains is the same passion that resided in his heart.

During the last period of his life, as in the last period of the painter Van Gogh's life, Micah was consumed by this passion which burned in him like a raging fire. The consequences, also like Van Gogh's, were tragic. Nonetheless, his passion still lives, — the same fervent passion that allowed the

73

Acadian people to persevere despite their sufferings and facing an uncertain future.

In 1764, by royal decrees, the Acadians were allowed to come back to their home as settlers, provided they swore allegiance to the Queen and became British subjects. Many accepted this bargain and we saw exiles come back to Acadie from the regions of the Saint Lawrence river, the Saint-Pierre-et-Miquelon Islands and the English colonies. Entire families formed caravans and crossed mountain ranges on foot, travelled through forests, crossed rivers, and braved all sorts of perils, suffering exhaustion and extreme deprivation. Month after month, wandering groups of gaunt, sorrowful people would trudge down the roads, struggling to reach the Promised Land.

This homecoming of the refugees inspired Henry Wadsworth Longfellow in 1847 to compose a moving poem titled *Evangeline*, read and cherished by all Acadians. It is the story of two lovers torn from each other at the time of the deportation who spent their lives searching for each other. The first verses carry us into the outstanding beauty of Acadie:

Ye who believe in this affection that hopes,
and endures, and is patient,
Ye who believe in the beauty and strength
of woman's devotion,
List to the mournful tradition still sung
by the pines of the forest;
List to a Tale of Love in Acadie,
home of the happy.
In the Acadian land, on the shores
of the Basin of Minas,
Distant, secluded, still,
the little village of Grand-Pré
Lay in the fruitful valley.
Vast meadows stretched to the eastward,
Giving the village its name,
and pasture to flocks without number.
Dikes that the hands of the farmers
had raised with labor incessant,

Shut out the turbulent tides,
but at stated seasons the floodgates
Opened, and welcomed the sea to wander
at will o'er the meadows.
West and South there were fields of flax,
and orchards and cornfields...

Thus dwelt together in love
these simple Acadian farmers —
Dwelt in the love of God and of man.
Alike were they free from
Fear that reigns with the tyrant,
and envy, the vice of republics.

Love for their native land was never uprooted from the hearts of the Acadian settlers. Their soul always lived in Acadie. Despite their misery and grief, the memories of their homeland were enough to nurture their dream of one day going back. Returning was harsh. But their courage wasn't in vain since those Acadians ensured the survival of their ethnic group. Forced to start over from nothing, miserable and without education, they lived in isolation and total abandonment. Only the purity of their moral values, their love of work, and a deep attachment to their faith in God, allowed the Acadians to restore the soul to this Acadie, which had been completely cut off from its founding families.

The story of the Acadians, strewn with disaster, is a model of courage. For me, this history continues through the lives of my children and of many of my fellow citizens.

Even if the Acadian presence in Quebec is not a well-known fact, no fewer than one million Quebecois can be considered to be of Acadian descent. Thousands of Quebecois have a last name of Acadian origin, but they usually never find out until they trace their genealogy. The poet Gilles Vigneault, the sculptor Louis-Phillipe Hébert, his two sons Henri and Adrien, writer Anne Hébert, and fashion designer Michel Robichaud, Maurice Richard, Jean Béliveau, Pierre Bourque, Montreal's former mayor... all of these well-known people have Acadian roots.

But the influence of Acadie goes beyond the celebrities. In Gaspésie, the towns of Bonaventure and Carleton as well as the village of Saint-Alexis, in the Matapedia valley, were founded by the Acadians. The same is true for the village of Saint-Grégoire of Nicolet whose Acadian influence can be found in many street names (we find there a Béliveau Street, a Landry Street, a Cormier Street, a Port-Royal Boulevard, and the Acadians Boulevard). The parish of Saint-Louis of Blandford, located in les Bois Francs, was also founded by the Acadians, as well as Wotton in the Eastern Townships. Also, the first inhabitants of Les-Iles-de-la-Madeleine were mostly Acadians, and in Kamouraska, we find a very Acadian agricultural technique: dikelands.

Back from their exile in Boston, numerous Acadians were welcomed in Lanaudière by the lords of Saint-Sulpice. These former deportees settled in "L'Achigan" (L'Épiphanie), in Saint-Sulpice, and mostly Saint-Jacques, which they founded and which were successively named Nouvelle-Acadie, Saint-Jacques-de-la-Nouvelle-Acadie, Saint-Jacques-de-l'Achigan, and finally Saint-Jacques-de-Montcalm. All the people of Lanaudière are very proud of their Acadian origin, and many of them still possess artifacts from the first Acadians settlers in the region.

The Acadian presence, in fact, can be felt throughout the province of Quebec. In the region of Chaudière-Appalaches, the village of Saint-Gervais still has an Acadian flag in its coat of arms, in remembrance of its founders. In Montérégie, Acadians back from exile in New England settled in the Richelieu Valley (Saint-Denis, Saint-Charles, Saint-Jean) and founded a parish called "L'Acadie." On the north shore of the Saint Lawrence river, archives tell the story of an important man, Napoléon Alexandre Comeau, an Acadian doctor, for whom the city of Baie Comeau was named.

It is clear that the Acadian people are very closely linked to the history of Quebec. But my greatest surprise was to discover that the founder of the village where I grew up, the priest Nicolas Tolentin Hébert, was also an Acadian.

So it is to an Acadian that Lac-Saint-Jean owes the foundation of its oldest parish, "Hébertville." It is in this little picturesque village, at the foot of a mountain range, covered with fir trees, that I spent the most beautiful moments of my childhood. My mother, now in her eighties, as well as my brother, my sisters, and their families are still living there at the present time. At the center of the village stands a tall monument honouring priest Nicolas Tolentin Hébert. He is standing beside a settler who is holding a woodcutter's axe on his shoulder. The arm of the priest is extended forward, pointing toward this fertile plain that became Lac-Saint-Jean county. What is striking to me are the eyes of the two men, looking as though staring into eternity, beyond the obstacles and difficulties, the sickness and plagues, the poverty and oppression — a gaze reaching beyond the centuries and generations, a gaze filled with hope …the Acadian look.

I leave the church of Saint Charles, deeply moved. With one last look at the magnificent stained glass work that illustrates the deportation. A red line runs through it. As if it were a torn page…blood…the red jackets of the British soldiers. It is said that on September 5th of each year, the rays of the noon sun reflect this line on the plaque commemorating Acadian history, located at the entrance of the little church. For me, this red line is forever engraved in my heart. Not one of resentment or vengeance toward the British and their descendents, but rather to cherish and honour this courageous people known as the Acadians.

Before leaving, I look at the guest book that invites visitors to leave their comments:

- Very good descriptions!
- Interesting!
- Great history.
- Beautiful place.
- Very beautiful gardens.
- Sad.
- A beautiful page of history.
- Good job.
- Cool.
- Lovely.

- Feeling proud – signed, Christian Bourque,
Petit Rocher, Acadie.

⇒≫≪⇐

Magnificent gardens embellish the site of Grand-Pré.
Thousands of multicolored flowers fill the warm summer air
with their perfume. Tall oaks shade the tired visitors who are
watching little ducks peacefully gliding on the water in the
pond. It is said that these oak trees are the only witnesses of
the good old days of Grand-Pré.

Near the church, at the center of the site, stands a monument to the memory of ancient Acadie. It is a bronze statue of
beautiful Evangeline, heroine of Longfellow's poem. We owe
the sculpture to Henri Hébert, a Quebec sculptor of Acadian
origin. The young peasant woman, wearing a long fringed
dress and bodice, walks along a dirt road or in a field, probably on her way to meet her fiancé, the handsome Gabriel. Her
head, tilted slightly backward, and her eyes looking toward
the sky and the distant horizon, suggests she is a dreamer. She
looks alive and victorious over the past centuries:

Benedict Bellefontaine, the wealthiest farmer
of Grand-Pré,
Dwelt on his goodly acres; and with him,
directing his household,
Gentle Evangeline lived, his child,
and the pride of the village.
Fair was she to behold,
that maiden of seventeen summers.
Black were her eyes as the berry that grows
on the thorn by the wayside,
Black; yet how softly they gleamed
beneath the brown shade of her tresses!
Sweet was her breath as the breath of kine
that feed in the meadows.
When in the harvest heat she bore
to the reapers at noontide
Flagons of home-brewed ale,
ah! Fair in sooth was the maiden.

I slowly walk around the statue. Astonishing is the face of Evangeline, seemingly displaying two different expressions. First, that of youthful optimism. It's the beautiful Evangeline, drunk with love, innocent and pure, already savouring the happiness she'll be experiencing in the arms of her beloved. But her face also expresses something resembling a tranquil strength. We recognize the traits of an older woman, sure of herself and of her own people. Her gaze is frank and peaceful. It is the gaze of a woman we'd ask counsel from, a woman we can confide in, one who will listen. A woman inspiring respect because she has overcome the trials of life.

Evangeline's right hand gently rests on her left hand. It's as if the hand that toiled the soil, ground wheat, soothed, dried tears, the hand of the older woman crossing centuries, was taking the young woman's hand, to tell her: "Take heart! You will make it! You will overcome!"

⇒⟩⟨⇐

I leave Grand-Pré. The scorching sun is slowly sinking, giving the cloudless sky its purple attire. Two bald eagles hover above a wheat field.

Before going back to the cabin, I want to see the place that one of Grand-Pré's tour guides pointed out to me: the place where the deportees boarded the ships on the day of the great deportation. I walk through a pasture where hefty milk cows graze peacefully; then, a cornfield where the stems reach twice my height. And between the edge of the cornfield and the Minas Basin lies a great dike, dividing the fertile land from the ocean's salty waters.

I walk silently along the dike, thinking of the brave men who built it. I want to walk where they walked. I feel like I am standing on holy ground; and, facing the setting sun, I pray for my children and for their yet unborn children. I pray that God would grant them the same courage that moved their Acadian ancestors and that they too would become builders of a better world.

Near the beach where once the small wooden boats landed, a great solitary oak stares at the open sea.

In the time of my confession,
in the hour of my deepest need
When the pool of tears beneath my feet
flood every newborn seed
There's a dyin' voice within me reaching out somewhere,
Toiling in the danger and in the morals of despair.

Don't have the inclination to look back on any mistake,
Like Cain, I now behold this chain
of events that I must break.
In the fury of the moment I can see the Master's hand
In every leaf that trembles, in every grain of sand.
Oh, the flowers of indulgence
and the weeds of yesteryear,
Like criminals, they have choked the breath
of conscience and good cheer.
The sun beat down upon the steps of time to light the way
To ease the pain of idleness and the memory of decay.

I gaze into the doorway of temptation's angry flame
And every time I pass that way I always hear my name.
Then onward in my journey I come to understand
That every hair is numbered like every grain of sand.

I have gone from rags to riches in the sorrow of the night
In the violence of a summer's dream,
in the chill of a wintry light,
In the bitter dance of loneliness fading into space,
In the broken mirror of innocence on each forgotten face.
I hear the ancient footsteps like the motion of the sea
Sometimes I turn, there's someone there,
other times it's only me.
I am hanging in the balance of the reality of man
Like every sparrow falling, like every grain of sand.

BOB DYLAN
(Album: Shot of Love)

Help!

THE SIGHS OF THE EXHAUSTED TRAVELLER mingle with the groans of the wounded man on his back. He's determined to go all the way, but the road is long and the burden increasingly overwhelming. He is weary. Feelings of failure and anguish are taking over. He knows that at any moment now, he himself may collapse.

—»><«—

At sunrise, I go to the sea. Waves gently caress the little black rocks around a ridge, which appears to be kneeling toward the ocean. Little by little, the mounting tide sends jets of liquid crystal to fill the miniature basins carved in the flat rock over the years. Watching the clouds roll by, lying on a huge, smooth rock, I sleep a little. When I wake up, the waves that were once rocking me to sleep have become enemies. The water is already covering the lower part of the rocky peak. It feels like I am besieged.

More stubborn than an army of soldiers, the waves attack me ferociously. They throw themselves against the rocks spitting their foam at me. Unrelenting, they give me no respite.

Around me, space is diminishing. I can still see the shore, but the rising tide has covered the beach, and the waters continue to rise. Completely at the mercy of this uncontrollable force, I have no choice but to wait for the tide to recede and for the waves to abandon their fight, backing off from me, bowing in defeat.

⇒≫⋘⇐

Assuming the role of a traveller who is carrying a wounded one on his shoulders is not an easy task. Neither is it always by choice that we find ourselves carrying someone else's burden. Life's circumstances sometimes direct us in such a way that we find ourselves, unwittingly, on a deserted island, having to help someone we love. Truly, not all travellers have the strength to carry the weight of a wounded one, and it is not uncommon for the traveller to find himself exhausted, without resources and losing hope.

This is why so many individuals and organizations offer support to those who are worn out and need a time of rest. The advantage of living in a society is that the strength of some can sometimes supplement the weakness of others.

Following Micah's death, I was often overwhelmed by waves of sadness and crashing waves of guilt. I would feel the need to be surrounded by people who loved me and in whom I could confide. Sadly, this need was not always met, and I often felt like a wandering traveller, carrying the burden of his sorrow alone, not knowing where to turn.

People I met wouldn't understand the depth of my suffering, of the feelings of my wounded love and the tragedy that this abrupt ending of the relationship with my son represented.

I expressed my grief to hard-hearted religious Pharisees, indifferent, and filled with prejudice toward me. Their attitude only contributed to compound my anxiety. I also searched for help from people pretending to abolish society's taboos but who became cold as soon as I mentioned God. Health professionals, refusing to allow him any room.

Like the traveller, I had to continue the walk, however painful. A determined traveller, but fragile. Fragile like all travellers …the lonely travellers.

I had to carry my burden alone. Added to the burden I was struggling with was my bitterness toward the health system and the doctors who could have saved Micah's life, if only they had paid more attention.

It is clear they lacked judgement or competence in their diagnosis and treatment. I made this sad discovery as I consulted the coroner's report. Here, verbatim, are the recommendations included at the end of the document:

> *"The Quebec Corporation of Medical Doctors* must acknowledge this report and, if they deem it necessary, inform the emergency room doctors of the delay in absorption of diphenhydramate through the stomach and gastro-intestinal tract, and advise a longer observation period for patients.

> *The Professional Services Department of the Centre Universitaire de Santé de l'Estrie, site Bowen*, must submit the report to the Committee on Causes of Death, in order for the committee to evaluate and submit their conclusions to the Council of Physicians, Dentists and Pharmacists, so that proper measures may be implemented to prevent other avoidable deaths."

This "avoidable" death was my son's! As I read those lines I was extremely angry. Micah would still be alive if he hadn't had to deal with a few incompetent people. I wanted to shout, shout to their face that they were not worthy of occupying positions for which they were so well paid. I wished that one day their own sick children would find themselves at the mercy of individuals as clumsy as they had been with my son so they would understand the gravity of their carelessness and the grief they had caused our family. I would have liked to see them stand trial and be condemned without mercy… and anger and hate started to grow in my heart and wreak havoc in my body.

In order not to be crushed by the weight of my bitterness, I decided to forgive rather than let these impulses destroy my soul. Losing Micah, watching my dreams and hopes of living beautiful moments with him die was affecting my daily life. I didn't want to vanish into the desert under the weight of events I could not change. So ...I screamed! I screamed my pain! I screamed my grief! I screamed to tell all those who were hurting that I also felt their sorrow!

I screamed, and the echo of my voice reached to the ends of the earth.

In order to end the bitterness, I chose to forgive. I had to avoid giving room to thoughts of curses, and instead I needed to nurture a correct attitude toward the medical profession. To do this, I initiated a book project that required the participation of doctors.

The project started after meeting a good friend of mine who practiced medicine for five years in an orphanage in Mexico. Nine more doctors gradually became involved in the project, and I'm proud to say we all became friends. The book that was the result of our work together, titled *Ten Quebec Doctors Talk about God*, is now distributed in many countries of the world.

I have to admit that the authenticity and honesty with which the authors of this book shared particular moments in their lives, successes, failures, and grief, has benefited me. Some of the topics particularly touched me. One of the authors chose to address the deficiencies of our health system even though he knew nothing of the neglect leading to Micah's death. Others touched on themes such as depression, suicide, and forgiveness.

The success of this project will never make me forget the circumstances surrounding my son's death and will never completely heal the wound that his tragic departure has caused. However, I know I made the right choice by letting forgiveness do its work in me.

A book in itself can never replace the affection of a friend and certainly not the comforting presence of God. But I know it can fill certain moments of solitude and contribute to the healing of those whose heart is in pain.

This fellowship in suffering, I experienced through the story a friend of mine – a psychologist and director of a shelter for women in crisis – was kind enough to share with me. She related an episode in the life of a person she highly esteems, her college sociology professor, Dr. Gary Leblanc. Dr. Leblanc and his family have, like me, crossed the horrible desert of their son's suicide. The text written by doctor Leblanc deeply moved me and helped me understand many important things that assisted me in my journey to healing.

It is with his permission that I respectfully quote his precious words in the following chapter. With all my heart, I hope they will be a source of comfort for you as they were for me.

A flood of grief,
Important lessons,
But still no answers
With regards to my son.

DR. GARY LEBLANC

WHEN THE DAM BREAKS

IT IS TRUE TO SAY that most of us are not leading the lives we planned. As a professional counsellor I had often seen evidence of that, yet I was personally, utterly unprepared for January 1999. Although my diagnosis of prostate cancer early in the month was a shock, it paled in comparison to the death of our eldest son, Shawn, on January 28, 1999, at the age of 27. Shawn was a wonderful, talented young man with tremendous potential. His untimely death dealt us a blow from which we will never fully recover.

Shawn was an excellent student, achieving the honour roll all through high school and graduating from Atlantic Baptist University ("ABU") with the highest standing in the graduating class. He received a full academic scholarship to Acadia University where he earned a Master of Arts in sociology. He was also an accomplished athlete, playing high school varsity basketball, football and rugby, of which he was team captain, and he was also captain of ABU's varsity basketball team. At ABU he rededicated his life to the Lord, served as chair of the sports committee, and in his senior year was a resident assistant, a key student-leadership position.

Enjoying adventure, he took a leave of absence from his job in Moncton and toured Europe on his own during May and June of 1998. He planned what became a marvellous odyssey, as he experienced so many different places and people.

It was his loving and gentle nature, however, that endeared him to everyone who knew him. Tutoring special students in school and helping problem children in Moncton's Special Care Homes demonstrated his concern for others, especially those less fortunate than he. It also illustrated his skill in relating to other people. At the time of his death, he was establishing his own retail business in Moncton and was on the verge of opening his store — a dream of his for some time.

What led him to take his own life on that fateful Thursday evening is still a mystery to us, his family, and to others who were close to him. We still struggle every day with the questions for which there seem to be no answers. He was a wonderful son and a loving friend, and an affectionate brother to Neil and Jaclyn. To our delight as parents, he often expressed his love for us; to have him go under such circumstances is incredibly difficult.

I could never have imagined how deep the hurt from the death of one's child could be until I experienced it myself. My wife, Peg, and I were literally sick to our stomachs for weeks after Shawn's death. The experience of grief was overwhelming, overshadowing everything else in our lives. One still must handle each day as it comes, for which God gives the strength, yet one lives with a constant sense of sadness that drenches all other realities. Even today, there are moments when the reality of what happened breaks through like water behind a crumbling dam, flooding the consciousness with the horror and trauma of that terrible day. Yet my most difficult struggle today is coping with what will never be. That I have no earthly future with Shawn is heartbreaking to contemplate. We will never again, in this life, share activities we both loved: our dreams, hopes, laughter, tears, a hug. We will never see a grandchild from our oldest son, who would have been a tremendous husband and father. I am haunted and saddened by the things that will never be. Each day I grieve for the things I did not say, and now can never say, to that precious person — and I wonder if it might have made a difference. The hope that helps sustain us is that we will be reunited with him in heaven, where he is now, with his heavenly Father.

This terrible tragedy, the sense of loss, the permanent ache in our hearts, has made us much more sensitive to tragic events in the lives of others. Just as being diagnosed and successfully treated for prostate cancer has sensitized me to the prevalence of this disease and to those who suffer from it, the death of Shawn has made me much more aware of the suffering of others. I realize now, as never before, that tragedy and pain happen to most of us, and for many, grief is their daily bread.

The notion that bad things happen only to bad people, or that bad things happen only to punish people for their evil deeds, is a lie. Yet these faulty perceptions go back a long way. When Jesus was asked who had sinned because a man had been born blind, he answered, "No one," which certainly stunned his first century audience (John, chapter 9). Indeed, we all know that sometimes the most wonderful people seem to have tremendous hardships and that, conversely, so often the "wicked prosper." Ecclesiastes 8:14 states that "There is something else meaningless that occurs on earth: righteous men who get what the wicked deserve." Even the apostle Paul had his afflictions, from which he was not relieved, and he had to realize that for him, as for us, God's grace is sufficient.

The past year has forced me to reflect on death, sickness, and evil in our world in a way I have never done before. Shawn's premature death was a horrendous tragedy, regardless of what positive learning may emerge because of it, and I am fully convinced that we should never ascribe good to evil. It is one thing to see that good may emerge from evil situations, but that is entirely different from believing that evil is actually good because of positive things that have resulted. As R.C. Sproul has said, even the assertion that "All things work together for good", in Romans 8:28, is a testimony to the triumph and power of God over real, death-dealing evil, not a signal that evil is really good in disguise.

Death and sickness, for example, are the result of sin and are not initiated by God "for our own good." Life is the gift of God, not death. I have been acutely gripped by the obscenity of death, just how terrible it can be. The death of a child, chronic illness, and horrific accidents — these are dreadful, and I believe that just as they break our hearts, they also break the heart of a loving God: "His heart is touched by our grief." Although such events are within his permissive will, they are not God's active will. The death of my beloved son Shawn will remain a terrible tragedy, regardless of the good that may emerge. God's sustaining power and provision are there for us when these terrible things happen, but these horrible events are the result of a fallen world, not the deliberate acts of a God bent on using evil to teach us lessons the hard way.

God's love, strength, comfort and grace are there for us to help us survive, and we will experience his presence when we need it most, but God does not beget evil to accomplish this in our lives. As we read in Job 34:10,12, "Far be it from God to do evil, from the Almighty to do wrong... It is unthinkable that God would do wrong." The Psalmist makes it very clear that our heavenly Father is "not a God who takes pleasure in evil" (Psalm 5:4).

Another new recognition for me is the incredibly wide-ranging impact of a tragedy. An individual or family tragedy affects friends, the church, the community, and so on, like ripples on a pond, washing over an ever-widening circle of people. I was amazed when confronted with the impact of Shawn's death. We, his immediate family, underwent incredible trauma and pain, but the hammer blow was also felt by our extended family, by Shawn's friends, family friends, the church, and the Atlantic Baptist University and Acadia University communities. We received responses from all over North America. The picture of his closest friends, fellow rugby players, strong, powerful men, weeping on our living room couch, unable to understand how one so loved could do such a thing, will stay with me all my life.

This ripple has significant implications for the way Christians are to minister in times of tragedy. Often we focus only on the immediate family. Yet there are others — sometimes many — who may actually need more help in coping as a result of specific personality strengths. Personalities vary tremendously, as do the environment and genetic endowments that have shaped them, equipping some to cope better than others.

At times I cope with pain and grief by increased activity and can express what I'm feeling to those close to me. My wife, Peg, on the other hand, tends to withdraw. Her activity level declines, and she becomes less expressive. We both are equally in pain, but we use different strategies to regain a sense of wholeness. Because people cope in different ways, they need to be ministered to in different ways. We must be sensitive to hurting people's individual character traits and to their own ways of handling grief and pain. In addition, the importance of friends, family, and trusted colleagues cannot be overstated. Loving support in times of terrible loss, pain, and grief can make all the difference.

The circumstances surrounding a sudden loss have much to do with the extent and depth of our grief. The expected death of an elderly person affects us very differently than the untimely death of a child. My diagnosis and treatment for cancer, and the death of Peg's mother two months after Shawn's death, were difficult. Yet they are more or less the norm for life and not totally unexpected. On the day after his death, one of my closest friends and I were driving back to Shawn's apartment, when Gordon commented how terribly unnatural this was, that our children are supposed to bury us, not us bury them.

I still feel off balance, these many months later. Shawn's death seems so out of sync with "normal" life, especially since he gave no visible warning of what was to happen — or none that we or his closest friends detected. Being unable to make any sense of what has happened as we grieve is incredibly oppressive; not only because of the loss of Shawn but also because of the method by which it happened.

Although I realize as never before that God works in ways that are far beyond my understanding and that his ways are not my ways (Roman 11:33), it is still very difficult to cope with the death of a son when it makes no sense. "Just leave it in the Lord's hands; he knows the future and the big picture," is easier said than done. It doesn't matter that I know

91

the statement is true. At times, I have been puzzled, hurt, angry, and doubtful as I experienced these events that seem so unfair, generating profound questions that may never be answered in my lifetime.

I have struggled deeply with questions such as: Where was the "friend that sticks closer than a brother" for Shawn that fateful evening of his death? What did Shawn feel? What was he thinking? How did he decide? Why, a thousand times why? I have no answers. I believe that God's ways are beyond my understanding and that our Lord is big enough to handle my doubts, questions, and even my anger. I believe that when we hit bottom, we have nowhere to go but to him, because in the end, as the disciples noted, only he has the words of eternal life. But I still have no answers about Shawn, and sometimes, like Jeremiah, I cry out (Jeremiah 12:1).

Even with all my questions, one of the most significant understandings arising from the horrific days of 1999 was to realize how God ministers to us when we are in terrible pain. God brings his strength, comfort, healing, and wholeness. He does not choose to use some supernatural zapping that energizes us and spirits away all the pain, hurt, doubt and sorrow. Instead, he uses people to accomplish this healing. Wonderful personal friends, family members, the marvellous faculty, staff, and students at ABU, the Hillside Baptist Church family, neighbours, and so many other caring people, have prayed, visited, sent cards and notes, letting the family know in wonderful ways that they were thinking of us and praying for us. If anything positive can come out of such a terrible event, it has been the marvelous reaction of so many people to our situation. God has used them to minister amazingly to our needs.

This is an important lesson. I realize as never before that I have the responsibility not only to pray for God's blessing for others in their time of tragedy, but also to be willing to be his instrument to help accomplish that blessing. Our tragedy — and I will always call it that — has created ministry opportunities that were previously unlikely. Doors have opened that I now can credibly walk through because of the recent events.

I have also learned that time may not be as good a healer as we may think. It has been well over a year since Shawn's death, and although some of the physical manifestations of the grief have eased, much of the horror of what happened is as present with me now as it was then. It is the same with others who suffer sudden, profound tragedy, and they too are sometimes simply overwhelmed with waves of pain and grief. So I learned that those who grieve may need our help for longer periods than I formerly recognized.

Yet, make no mistake — I would trade all the opportunities that have emerged and all that I have learned if I could reverse what happened. The good that has come from this tragedy has not outweighed the bad, and it never will in this life. I miss my son. I wish he were here today. But… it did happen, and God has allowed me opportunities for ministry which were previously unimaginable, to help diminish the hurtful consequences.

When all is said and done, however, God is still there, and his grace is sufficient even in these terrible times. We have not been abandoned, even though it may feel that way. His love is still available for strength and comfort. His presence, as he promised, never fails. This must be our hope and strength. Without this hope, all is lost, and life is meaningless and not worth living. We either live in hope or we die in despair. To know his presence is with us each day gives each day meaning and provides us with the courage to face the future with hope.

⟫⟪

During one of my trips to New Brunswick, I stopped in Moncton to spend some time with Dr. Leblanc. I wanted to thank him and tell him how much I appreciated the text he wrote.

And I didn't regret it. As he opened his office door, his eyes told me that I was welcome and understood. Here I was, sitting in conversation with a man who had experienced a tragedy similar to mine, in this place, where, a few months earlier, Shawn had come to visit and bring back the books he had borrowed, before he ended his life.

On one of the bookcases, I noticed a photograph of a happy, peaceful family. I see Shawn for the first time: a tall, handsome young man, with bright eyes and a happy smile. Then Dr. Leblanc drew my attention to a painting Shawn had bought while travelling in Europe. It is the picture of a golfer. His son purposefully chose it, knowing his father loved playing golf.

We talked for a long time, taking turns sharing about our lives, our sorrows, our questions and our individual feelings. We didn't formulate great theories about suicide, nor did we come up with answers to our questions. We simply talked, and I think we felt true compassion for one another.

I know Dr. Leblanc must have been overloaded with work on that day, as it was the beginning of the school year. So it touches me even more that he took the time to meet with me. This meeting enabled me to understand how helpful it is for human beings who go through the same kind of trials to meet and share their feelings. It is not always easy, particularly for us men, who have the reputation of repressing our feelings instead of sharing them. But believe me, it is worth the effort!

When I saw him last
he had that look in his eyes
I said, 'Do you need to talk?'
he said, 'No.'
So I called him up, asked him again
and I waited a while —
he began to speak, then he started to cry

You know some things are best left unspoken
and some things just never work out
and sometimes, seems you try and you try
and whatever you do
There's a fix that you're in,
and you just can't get out
he said, 'I need your help,
I need it now
Give me the strength to go on'

PHIL COLLINS
(Released as B-side of 'We Wait And We Wonder' CD single, 1994)

SIMPLE FAITH

As Dr. Francine Nicloux writes in the book *Ten Quebec Doctors Talk about God*: "Nothing belongs to us: neither life nor death nor health nor our future. The only thing that belongs to us is the way that we act or react, knowing that God is always there to bless, support and teach us. The only reality is that our life on earth is very short compared to eternity."

Dr. Nicloux expressed this thought following a time of trial that she and her family went through. Their son Jérémie, age sixteen, suddenly found himself afflicted with a sickness, the consequences of which could have been tragic. Fortunately, through medical means, they were able to reverse the condition and Jérémie recovered.

The struggles we go through can help us discover a side of God previously unknown to us. Despite the fact that God became the target of many undeserved accusations (as if he were to blame for human suffering), he nonetheless became for many the source of support and comfort they so needed, in times when their own strength failed them.

Unfortunately, the variety of vaguely "spiritual" philosophies, "holy" wars, the abuse committed by certain members of the clergy, and the unrelenting harassment by sects have created a climate of suspicion and confusion in our society. Spirituality has become a reality that many wish to avoid at any cost.

There is more to it, however, than that sad track record! The roots of the Christian faith run deep in our culture's history and beyond, into the history of the human race. One has only to look at the lives of Francis of Assissi, John-Sébastian Bach, Dr. Albert Schweitzer, Mother Theresa, or, more recently, into the farewell letter former minister Camille Laurin wrote his wife before crossing eternity's threshold, to recognize the imprint God still leaves on people.

Faith can be a powerful source of support. The reason many react with indifference, even disgust, when they hear the name of Jesus Christ, is that too often religion has been used to exert pressure or to promote causes that have nothing to do with God. And so it is important today that we distinguish between man-wielded religion and God's authentic love.

In some religious circles, divorcees are still treated as if they were part of an inferior class. They are forbidden to sit on pastoral boards, and they are kept from activities that would allow them to address crowds. Meanwhile, their financial contributions are welcomed with open arms. I can quote the case of a church that turned away a man whose son just committed suicide on the pretext that they didn't have the maturity to accept people with such "problems." Another church closed its doors on a young man who had confided in his pastor regarding his struggles with homosexuality, asking for help. With such an awful attitude, it is not surprising that churches are empty instead of thronging with hurting people who are thirsting for true faith.

In today's society psychologists and social workers have replaced the priests. People go to them to be absolved of their guilt. I myself have encountered a few counsellors who displayed such an incredibly cold approach because they thought their knowledge of psychology could replace love and respect, essential elements to a true healing of the soul.

The tragedy with many counsellors is that in trying to counter the sometimes toxic effects of man's religion, they have suppressed the idea of God himself. Many have turned to New Age philosophies. Others to atheism. The problem in taking God out of the picture, is that we also eliminate certain

Biblical values, which are essential to the smooth functioning of society.

In the province of Quebec, where I live, turning away from Biblical values has had catastrophic results. According to social ratings, people in Quebec are among the most unhappy people on earth. For many years, Quebec has had the highest suicide rate among youth. These sad statistics now extend to the 19-to-40 year-old group, so much so that in a recent article in the *Journal de Montréal*, it was stated that 1999 broke all records for youth suicide in Quebec. Suicide is now, and by far, the highest unnatural cause of death in our province. Suicide now claims twice as many victims as traffic accidents.

Quebec also holds the world record for the number of abortions, with 27.6% of pregnant women in Quebec ending their pregnancy through abortion. Statistics Canada recently published figures that show an increase in this tendency. Another record is the number of births out of wedlock, 54.3% of children being born to unwed couples, twice the number observed in other provinces. Moreover, our birth rate in 1998 was 1.45 children per woman, while the experts claim that 2.1 is required simply to maintain our population. Again, Quebec lags behind other provinces.

Further, of all the Canadian provinces, Quebec has the highest rate of emigration. In other words, there are more people leaving Quebec than there are coming in. Even with the present quota of 30,000 immigrants per year, we will not be able to compensate for the citizens we are losing. Are we, as a people, about to disappear?

Eleanor Roosevelt once said:

He who loses money loses much.
He who loses a friend loses more.
He who loses faith loses everything.

Wouldn't it be wise to recognize our mistakes and turn to God and the Bible in order to become a prosperous and happy nation once again?

One day an expert in religious law stood up to test Jesus by asking him this question:

"Teacher, what must I do to receive eternal life?" Jesus replied, "What does the law of Moses say? How do you read it?"

The man answered, "You must love the Lord your God with all your heart, all your soul, all your strength, and all your mind. And, love your neighbour as yourself."

"Right!" Jesus told him. "Do this and you will live!"

The man wanted to justify his actions, so he asked Jesus: "And who is my neighbour?"

Jesus replied with an illustration:

"A Jewish man was traveling on a trip from Jerusalem to Jericho, and he was attacked by bandits. They stripped him of his clothes and money, beat him up, and left him half dead beside the road.

By chance a Jewish priest came along; but when he saw the man lying there, he crossed to the other side of the road and passed him by. A temple assistant walked over and looked at him lying there, but he also passed by on the other side.

Then a despised Samaritan came along, and when he saw the man, he felt deep pity. Kneeling beside him, the Samaritan soothed his wounds with medicine and bandaged them. Then he put the man on his own donkey and took him to an inn, where he took care of him.

The next day he handed the innkeeper two pieces of silver and told him to take care of the man.

"If his bill runs higher than that," he said, "I'll pay the difference the next time I am here."

"Now which of these three would you say was a neighbour to the man who was attacked by bandits?" Jesus asked. The man replied, "The one who showed him mercy."

Then Jesus said, "Yes, now go and do the same."

In my book *Ten Quebec Doctors Talk about God,* my friend Dr. Alain Bérubé established an interesting parallel between science and faith. Here is what he says:

> I believe that prayer and medicine are very complementary.
> Unfortunately, spirituality has been taken out of medicine,
> particularly from psychiatry.
> We know that people need more than antidepressants.
> They often need to be listened to, accepted, surrounded,
> and comforted either by a spouse, a family member
> or a psychiatrist.
> Although this type of intervention contributes to their healing,
> it never or rarely provides a complete cure for the illness. But
> why stop there?
> Another dimension to life is the spiritual dimension. And this
> dimension is the one which gives real meaning to life.
> Many of my patients go through a crisis in their lives. They
> question their very existence on this earth. They know very
> well that all is not material and that the spiritual side exists.
> Why then should we not take this spiritual dimension into
> account in the process of helping them?

Discovering the love and forgiveness of God is always a source of healing. There are no parameters for what we could call "limits to God's love." The love of God is infinitely more immense than the ocean and his forgiveness can reach to the deepest abyss.

The Bible tells us that one day Jesus sat at the table of an important, well-respected man. During the meal, a prostitute came to Jesus and bathed his feet with her tears. To the host, this woman was society's garbage and her presence embarrassed him. Or maybe he himself had been one of her clients, and feared that his guests would learn of it!

Like the indifferent character in Micah's sketch, this respectable man had a heart of stone. However, Jesus could read not only his heart, but also hers. He knew that the many men who took advantage of this woman offered only bitterness in return. He understood that her situation was hopeless. He knew that rather than choosing to end her life, she chose to come and cry at his feet. "I forgive you," said Jesus, gently stroking her beautiful hair, "Go and sin no more." This woman went away freed from her sins, but the host remained prisoner of his.

God's forgiveness accomplishes miracles in the lives of those who come to him. We are surrounded by examples.

I heard the testimony of a group of young people who, in their desire to help the broken people of their town, rented a hall above a tavern. They invested their own savings to make the place welcoming, and they bought small tables, a good sound system, and they invited local artists for evenings of contemporary music and Christian testimonies.

Frequently, many of the tavern patrons, drawn by the music, came upstairs, drink in hand. One of them was known in the whole neighbourhood as the town drunk. From morning to night, he could be seen staggering on the sidewalk. His health had so deteriorated that his doctor gave him only a few months to live. One day, as he was sitting at one of the tables on the second floor, one of the young Christians felt compassion for this stranger. He even felt deep inside that he had something like a message from the Lord, a message he had to give to this poor drunk.

He immediately consulted one of the pastors who decided to go with him to talk with the man and the three of them started a conversation. Even though the man couldn't understand everything, the young man shared the message God had placed in his heart: "Dear sir, it seems that our heavenly Father would like to tell you that he has compassion for you. He loves you and understands your grief for he also witnessed the death of his only son."

On hearing this, the old alcoholic broke into tears and for many hours nobody could comfort him.

What the young Christian didn't know was that this man had once been prosperous and happy. One day, his one son ran into the room where he was resting, holding a firearm that he had taken from the closet. The father knew that this rifle was never left loaded and that the bullets were well hidden. The idea came to him to play cowboys and Indians with his son. What he didn't know was that his son had found the ammunition and had loaded the gun. The father pulled the trigger and saw his child's head explode before his very eyes. Unable to forgive himself for such negligence, he fell into the deepest of despair and alcoholism.

But after years of horrible torment, this suffering man found himself sitting at a table in a café listening to the words that God was speaking to him through a young man. All at once the sufferings of the past came to the surface, and he broke down sobbing. Soon his heart was filled with the love and forgiveness of God that was flowing in him like a healing river. Not only were his heart and soul healed, but also a medical visit revealed that his stomach and liver had also been miraculously healed. He stopped drinking and found happiness again.

We have to admit that in some cases only God can intervene and bring the dead back to life. Moreover, love always restores hope. It is astonishing to see how people who go through difficult trials develop a particular understanding for others who are experiencing similar struggles.

I met a young Peruvian woman who immigrated to Canada after going through difficulties in her country. After many years of effort and perseverance, she completed a master's degree in psychology in order to work helping young Canadians. In addition to spending long hours on her homework, she volunteered at a center for distressed youth and runaways. The theme of her thesis was the behaviour of prisoners incarcerated in state prisons, and, more specifically, the case of an individual named Carl.

Carl was from a dysfunctional family. When he was four, Carl's father, who was a violent criminal, vowed to murder his mother's new boyfriend. As a result, his mother left town, abandoning Carl and severing all family ties.

Carl was taken to his grandparents. He visited his father in prison regularly, totally clueless about the real situation his father was in. He was told that his father, his hero, was in the army and that the prison was really his headquarters.

When Carl was a teenager he learned the truth about his father's crimes and violence, in particular against police officers. He continued to visit him in prison and even succeeded in sneaking some drugs in for him.

By the time he was fifteen, Carl was disgusted with life and thought about suicide. His future appeared like a black hole before him. He was convinced that sooner or later he would be murdered. At age sixteen he met his mother again, but this attempt at reuniting only lasted four months. At seventeen, he took part in two crimes with his father who was in and out of prison. One of these crimes involved a kidnapping. The ordeal ended badly: the police found Carl and his father, hiding in a motel. There was an exchange of gunfire. His father was badly wounded in the leg after shooting a police officer.

At eighteen, during a fight with his girlfriend, Carl hit a policeman and ended up behind bars. He was again put in prison, at twenty years old. This time, though, he was served a sentence of thirteen years for assault, theft and kidnapping.

Carl's life as a prisoner wasn't always easy, and he was regularly sent to the isolation cell because of his bad behaviour. Living with criminals, Carl became hardened, his heart bruised and wounded. One day, however, he knelt down in his cell and asked God to save him. His cry of distress was heard and he felt incredible peace, a peace he had never felt before. It was the beginning of a new life.

For Carl, no more isolation cell, for the prison chapel became his new home. He learned to read the Bible and to know God. He also met a young volunteer who from time to time came to visit the prisoners, encouraging them and sharing her faith in God. This young volunteer later became his wife.

Carl and Rose have now been married for fourteen years and have three beautiful children. Upon his release from prison, he became director of a homeless shelter and is working actively rehabilitating former prisoners. When I met Carl, he was exactly as I had imagined, a simple man, warm and smiling, riding a motorcycle. He was happy to give me a tour of his new facility.

Carl continued his relationship with his father, but now he also prayed for him. He didn't always believe it was possible for such a man to be converted and to experience change in his life, but he kept on praying.

An event that occurred in his father's life allowed Carl to see that his prayers were not in vain. During one of his many incarcerations, three prisoners made their way to the father's cell intending to murder him. One was armed with a stick, another one with a knife. The third one was supposed to stand watch while his accomplices carried out their plan. The first man hit him on the head with the stick, but when the other one tried to stab him in the stomach, he was incapable of doing so. An invisible force was holding his arm back. Filled with fear, the three men ran away. Carl's father recognized the goodness of God towards him and surrendered his life into the hands of Jesus Christ.

Carl and his father visit periodically, but for them everything has changed. Gradually, Carl's father has been allowed to spend short periods of time outside of prison, under supervision …provided he stays with his son!

Are there situations too complex or too desperate for God to intervene? Are there hearts so hard they cannot be penetrated by divine compassion? These stories convince me that there are not.

For many long months, however, my own experience convinced me of the contrary!

The Man with A
Heart of Stone

Solitary, austere, desert stork,
I'm death stoked.
Rock, burning, your rudeness is ice.
If at least I could lean on your stout roughness,
To rest, to breathe,
Renew my strengths,
To calm my tensed muscles.
I approach, I touch you,
I get wounded.
The brute stone of your body bites my flesh
Already burning...
You hurt me,
Not even looking at me.
My sweat pours, I crumble...
You don't see me.
Proud, eyes fixed on the horizon,
But the sand has furrowed your face
and turned your eyes to stone
You don't hear my cry for help
Nor the poorly articulated words
Tearing from my throat.
Your ear shut,
Like madhouse steel doors,
Impassable for the wretch
Held captive
Away from human compassions,
Only hope for healing.
You confuse tender and weak,
You're as dry as a dried-up river bed,
Unable to help the one dying of thirst.
What you thought a strength has become a prison.
Your heart a fortress no one can conquer,
Stone statue,
Your soul has left.

C.T.

FOUR PARENTS

IN VAIN I TRIED TO ERASE from my consciousness the morbid image of this man. Alas, he haunts my days and disturbs my sleep. I can't do anything about it. An acute feeling of failure mixed with guilt pierces my soul. My fear turns into darkness, my thoughts drift away. My strength melts away like a candle and dark walls rise around me like a prison where I'm hiding to avoid insanity. I crumble. Too weak to scream, mute, my anguish takes over. This distress, this sadness, this darkness assaults me, trying to conquer and annihilate me.

I have no alternative other than to face this man with the heart of stone. I have to look at him intensely and accept the verdict. And since destiny forces Micah's death on me, I also must embrace this hideous and repulsive man. This man with a heart of stone, insensitive, unable to do anything whatsoever to change the distress that surrounds him and unable to find a solution to the problems confronting him. To change and become a better man is a foreign concept to him.

I am now looking at this disgusting character, paralysed, fatalistic, gazing at his fellow companions in misery but ignoring their call for help. For him there exists no solution. His nonchalance bears witness to his long walk in the desert, much too long. There he lost hope. He lost his way, and never found it again. He is the sole source of his own misfortune. When his eyes scan the horizon, it is not in the hope of seeing help come to him, but rather in anticipation of being swallowed up completely and forever by the next storm.

If at times he looks toward the two men beside him, it is to assess how they are disturbing "his peace." No word of comfort, no compassionate silence. When he opens his mouth, it is to affirm the finality of fate.

No! That's enough! I do not want to be like this man! I will fight to the bitter end to offer comfort to the wounded and afflicted who wander across my path. This heart of stone has to break!

If you knew, Micah, how much your sketch reaches my soul. If you knew how much your truthfulness breaks my chains…

…If you knew how much I miss you.

-->><<--

It is raining today. Small droplets gently sliding down the cabin roof, the first to welcome me to this new day. The air is fresh. Wrapped in my multicoloured quilt, I place a few logs in the old wood stove to light a fire. The cabin now warm, I put my raincoat on and go for a walk, down one of the small trails. The breeze from the mountain intoxicates me. The fragrance exuding from the fir trees and the pines, mixed with that of the grass, carries me to a faraway land.

I picture my father, Médéric, walking softly ahead of me, his hunting rifle on his shoulder, slowly making his way around the trees, looking for hare and partridge. How magical those moments are for a seven-year old youngster wanting to learn to hunt in the company of his hero, his father. At the end of the day when we had a few birds in the bag, he would place an old can on a tree stump and, with great care, would place his rifle in my hands, making sure he also offered support to my shoulder to counter the shock of firing. It was a solemn moment for this little David Crockett who spent all his time reading the adventures of Kit Carson, Roy Rogers, Buffalo Bill and Geronimo.

Pow! I killed a buffalo! My target flies in the air… not surprisingly …we were just using buckshot.

Each tree in the forest seems to echo a multitude of memories: The tall, white, birch trees whose bark often found its way into my art books in primary school; the rich clusters of little orange berries suspended from the branches of mountain ash bring me back to the living room of my house in Amqui, where I watched the red-winged blackbird feeding, and where later I would watch my children play in the street.

The raspberry bushes along the path bring me back to my childhood. I can remember holding a plastic cup tightly in my little hands, and my father, at regular intervals, would drop the big red berries into it. They would quickly find their way into the little picker's mouth. I think of the pies my mother baked every time I go to Hébertville. She's the best pie-maker in the world! And even if my four sisters excel at cooking today, none of them has quite discovered the secrets of this eighty-two year old grandmother.

The forest reminds me of my father. For years he worked as a lumberjack. He knew all the legends and stories of that kingdom: the talking bears, the violin-playing hares, the dancing raccoons. My brother and I marvelled as dad told us these stories.

But the deep love I had for my father didn't keep us from constantly fighting when I was in my early teens. Then he left this world. I was only fourteen. Talking about his death brings confused memories. At that time, it seems I failed to express appropriate emotions in a lot of situations and moods. I expressed cold indifference in situations that should have deeply affected me. When father died, for example, I couldn't shed a tear.

At fourteen, in full-fledged identity crisis, I had observed that most of the men didn't cry when they stood before my father's coffin, even though they were his friends. In those days, everyone believed that "men don't cry!"

I attributed my emotional confusion to the hardness of my heart. I even wet my eyes with water and rubbed them in order to make them red, so that no adult would think I was insensitive. Nobody ever explained to me that people react differently to trauma, and that tears come later for some. I then judged myself as being a hypocrite at my own father's death. How confused I was!

I clearly remember the moment he left the house for the last time to go to the hospital. The old lumberjack stood near the door. As usual, his brown eyes were warm and loving, albeit a hint of sadness could be detected. I think he knew he wasn't coming back. Though my father wasn't very educated, he knew the language of nature. I remember him telling my grandfather that he could discern when it was time for horses to leave this world, just by the look in their eyes. I think Médéric knew on that day, as he left the house, that he was leaving it for the last time. And he was right.

But I never forgot his eyes, so filled with affection! And my father's loving gaze stayed with me all through my troubled teens and my adult life. Even my twisted perception of certain realities, interpreted through my guilty and tormented emotions, has never erased the imprint of his love. And when, as happens with many people, my father's vision weakened with age, he could still perceive the unseen with clarity. During the worst of my rebellious years, I felt he could see through my troubled adolescent heart. He could see the sorrow and turmoil of my immature nature, as I sought to confront an adult world, while still attached to childhood.

My parents didn't have a lot of money but loved each other dearly. As was common in Quebec at that time, families were large. Many children were born to them, two boys and seven girls. Then another little boy arrived, this one adopted from an orphanage ...it was me!

At the time when they decided to adopt a child, their family consisted of five girls (two more boys and one girl had died at an early age or at birth). My brother Gilles was born one year after my adoption.

My father had been in charge of a lumberjack work camp where men worked hard and liked to go for a drink when they got back to town. In fact, they liked to go for many drinks! At that time my father deeply wished to have a son, and he and my mother were thinking about adoption. But feminine wisdom required of Médéric that he first give up alcohol altogether. He accepted. My mother waited one year before initiating the preliminary process of adoption to be certain that her husband would keep his promise. He held to it and never broke it.

He was forty-six years old and my mother thirty-six when they adopted me. And I was three months old when they came to the orphanage in Chicoutimi to get me. It didn't matter how many times they repeated the story — they were always happy to tell it to me, and their faces lit up each time. Of dark complexion and very thin, I was not, at first, very attractive. What caused my father to choose me from among the others was the ready smile I gave him when he looked at me. And he welcomed me into his arms, and under his roof.

My parents were good parents, but sometimes I would oppose the values they taught me, creating crises and conflicts. Nevertheless, their love was unconditional. My father had a booming voice and we could easily hear him when he was talking with his friends at the smith forge, more than 600 feet from our house. His language was coloured with swear words.

I would at times be playing at the other end of the village when suddenly my father's voice, piercing through the sound barrier, would let me know it was time to come home. I could by times negotiate a few minutes' reprieve, on warm summer nights when we played hide and seek, but doing it a second time in the same evening was out of the question! Obedience was not an option in our home, but a virtue often learned through the seat of our pants. Tucked away in one the kitchen drawers was the source of my woes, a leather strap about ten centimeters wide which my parents used to remind me that there was someone in charge, and there were rules to follow. I often took and hid this cursed object before realizing that my father's warehouse was full of them. He only had to step out to the barn and come back with his new leather ally, thicker, more flexible, and more dreaded. It was impossible to escape it!

My father never hit me in the face, as his goal wasn't to humiliate me but to conquer the ungratefulness and lack of discipline that sought to take root in my life. This form of correction does not necessarily work with all children, but as a general rule, I consider it was profitable for me. Times and methods have changed when it comes to disciplining children, but I am happy that my parents succeeded in teaching me principles of honesty and respect.

I did my best to pass these same principles on to my children and I can see the good results in their lives. However, I consider that in their case, physical punishment was not the best method. I am not a violent man but I feel that there were a few times when I went too far. Even though my children know I love them and want the best for them, I have asked their forgiveness for the times my discipline was too severe.

I often saw my own father kneel at the foot of his bed, without aid of the rosary or a statue. I truly believe he was talking to God. His face hidden in his rough hands, he was probably offering to the Almighty his sorrows, his worries, his unsuccessful attempts to reason with his adopted son who was now a teenager. His prayers were not in vain, even if he didn't live long enough to see them answered. If my father were still with us, I know he would be proud of his Claude, as he would also be of all his children. I also know that I will see him again some day at that great feast in the hereafter. What a marvellous day it will be!

I really love going back to the village where I grew up. Each visit to the family house brings back a host of happy memories. I see myself again, as a small child, hiding under the big veranda, listening to the rain falling on the leaves of the beautiful maple tree which stretched its branches over a portion of my parents' large garden. I remember harvest time, helping my father pick carrots, beets, turnips, potatoes, corn and "gourganes," a type of bean particular to the Lac-Saint-Jean region.

I remember the white lilies growing on the fence along the sidewalk, and the hundred bouquets I'd pick for my mother. I also remember the huge milk drums our neighbour farmer would carry to the cheese factory in town, in his old truck. I remember the little river on the secondary country road and its water, so pure we could drink it. I probably caught my first trout in this river.

I remember the bitter aroma of the soap our other neighbour, Mrs. Allard, used to make, and her ten dogs that would never stop barking whenever we came close to her house.

I can still hear the hammer ringing on the blacksmith's anvil and the whistling saws of the mills where they cut the logs. I hear the happy shouts of my friends as they played in the street after supper, while parents talked politics on the porch.

I hear the guitar and accordion melodies played at our family reunions at Christmas and New Year's. I can still see my nephews, my nieces, and myself, laughing, dancing, and binging on multicoloured sandwiches that my sister had prepared for the occasion. I see father giving us the traditional blessing, a beautiful tradition that my mother continued!

I see our cabin on the shore of Lac-à-la-Croix and all those magnificent sunny days, the swimming, the boat rides, the sing-alongs in the evenings around the campfire, and the light dancing in our eyes.

What a great privilege to have been adopted by such good parents and to live in such a close-knit family where harmony endures to this day. What comfort to still be able to share with my mother my joys and my sorrows, to pray with her and read passages from the Bible with her. The older I get, the more I understand what a precious treasure my adopted family is.

Some years ago, however, I began to search for my birth parents. After a few months, I received a call from an agency telling me that my efforts were successful and that they had recently found my mother. I was happy. All we had to do was arrange a meeting. A few years earlier I had received information on the background of my birth parents. I learned that my mother's mental health was fragile, that she suffered from epilepsy and that she had spent time on a psychiatric ward. This information saddened me but intensified my desire to meet her. I discussed my plans with Albertine, my adoptive

mother, to make sure she understood and supported my decision. She encouraged me to go ahead.

And then the big day arrived!

I was to meet my mother in front of the senior citizens'
residence where she lived. I felt both anxious and fragile.
When the door opened and I saw this beautiful, smiling,
sixty-three year old lady with silver hair, coming towards me,
there rose in me a feeling that is difficult to describe. It was
as if profound and intimate bonds came to life between this
stranger and me before we even shared a single word. We
spent the whole afternoon together. I realized she suffered
from slight loss of memory but it did not affect her lucidity or
her sense of humour. During our subsequent encounters, I
came to understand the rocky path that Claudette had travelled. She didn't give me many details regarding her father
except that he was an alcoholic. I don't think she stayed with
him for very long after her mother died.

She, in turn, then married an alcoholic who beat her and
committed adultery with a neighbour. Before this marriage,
however, Claudette had become pregnant during a brief affair
with a married bartender. Traumatised by the situation, she
sought professional help who decided she needed psychiatric
care because of her state of depression. She was institution-
alised with mental patients and although she was not supposed to stay more than two weeks, it turned out to be a two-
and-a-half-year nightmare. My heart sank when I learned that
Claudette spent her entire pregnancy in the psychiatric hospital and that many times she tried to abort the child she was
carrying.

She couldn't look at me when she got to that painful part
of her story, our story. For all those years, this enormous burden had weighed on her conscience. I understood she needed
to talk about it, that she needed to be freed from it. I took her
hand in mine and, through my tears, I forgave her with all my
heart. We then prayed together, asking God to wash over us
with his love and healing. When I went back to see Claudette
some time later, I noticed a positive change in her. Her coun-

tenance was brighter and she was more at ease. We went out for a meal together.

Later, I began to search for my birth father. This time, it wasn't long before I found myself face to face with my father, a handsome man, strong, well built, tanned, and looking ten years younger than his actual age. He had worked in bars for the greater part of his life and had gone through a divorce. He also told me that he had been a boxing champion and that he had practiced karate until he was seventy-one years old. He was then seventy-eight and had suffered a heart attack shortly before our first meeting. We were both very happy to find each other.

I still visit him from time to time. I like to be in the presence of good old Gerry. But I can see a deep sadness in his eyes. Maybe it comes from remorse for the life he led, and finding himself alone and facing imminent death. I pray with all my heart that he may discover the infinite love and forgiveness of the Saviour. I earnestly desire for him to find the peace that only Jesus can bring to his soul.

I am happy to have met Gerry and Claudette, but their presence can never be compared to the years my adoptive parents gave to me. I can say I love them all but the intensity of my love is not the same for them all. Nothing could replace the love that Médéric and Albertine lavished on me day after day throughout my childhood and adolescence. All my life I will be grateful to them for this. I also love Gerry and Claudette, but our relationship still has to grow. For now, I fully appreciate the privilege of enjoying good times with them.

As the bark surrounds the sap,
So my arms enfolded her
All day long ...and maybe all night too.

She was neither sick, nor sad, nor wounded,
I watched over her and she hardly moved,
As the sap beneath the bark.

And then, she was gone.
And my arms, stunned with her fragrance,
Kept on embracing her...

When I lifted my eyes,
A tree reborn I was,
Every leaf renewed...

FELIX LECLERC

THE LITTLE BIRD FEEDER

ALL THE TREES IN THE FOREST wave at me like old friends as I walk by. Their branches join hands above my head, forming a canopy over the narrow path that takes me to the sea. Their leaves are already blushing with the first colours of autumn, just as I, too, in my mid-forties, gradually display the first colours of the autumn of my life.

And my thoughts, once more, turn toward my son.

After his departure, my heart endlessly sought after him in my memories ...there were fleeting images I could never really lay hold of ...the horror! Like an old computer whose data had been corrupted, my heart "crashed." All the information stored in my thoughts was vanishing as if attacked by a computer virus. The only thing I knew for certain was that somewhere in my memory there was a host of preserved information that I was unable to access. No more windows to the past. Only invisible files, prisoners of a system that even emotions could not enter.

The tragedy of Micah's death had upset my memory until time and the goodness of God gradually repaired the terrible damage. There came that morning when, on the sidewalk, I crossed paths with a young man of about sixteen, who strangely resembled Micah. I was at once transported into another world, the world of my memories. On another occasion, it was through a melody I heard amidst the bustling city noises: a melody from a long time ago, which, by chance,

119

came discreetly to open the door of my heart. It was as if a spring wind had invaded my house with its fragrance, allowing Micah to live again for a moment in my thoughts, and I deeply savoured each of those precious moments.

These memories sometimes resurface at very unexpected times.

I am in the basement of the building where I live, a dark and humid place. I am in the process of moving out, and I have to sort the contents of a few boxes. Things are in a mess and the smell isn't pleasant. I quickly open and close each box, putting aside the things I want to get rid off, such as dishes, old books, fishing gear, skates with rusted blades, ski boots, video tapes, and a game of Monopoly forgotten there for years.

I pick up a small dusty box, open it, and for a moment the earth stands still. I am paralysed. Tears stream down my dirty cheeks. Without a word, without a sound, unable to fight, I surrender to this wave of memories that washes over me. It is impossible to describe this sacred moment, this force of emotion that brings me into the presence of my beloved child. This power transcends reason. Inundated by these moments of intimacy that reconcile my present sorrow to my past happiness, my wounded soul bathes in the anointing of a balm that soothes and heals. Within the box, two little pieces of grey wood joined together in the middle by a piece of scotch tape. On one of them, a flower, painted with oil paints. A colourful flower in full bloom. The violet, rose and white entwined amidst splashes of pastel yellow.

I pull this work of art out of its cardboard box. It is a little wooden trough, a bird feeder. Micah built it for me and had given it to me as a gift. It was very pretty, like a quaint little house. One side of the roof opens up to allow for birdseed to be placed inside. The base is lined with small openings, giving the birds access to the food. A series of small, white, wooden pegs support the roof and form a perch. The pegs are linked together by small wooden cubes painted black. I recognize the skill and ingenuity of my son. He had evidently taken great pleasure in constructing this little masterpiece.

But why a bird feeder? He could have built a small chest to store the thousand and one knick-knacks lying around the workshop. He could have invented a new type of pencil case with built-in pencil sharpener and kept it for himself! He could have come up with dozens of inventions, all very useful. But he decided to build a bird feeder. He built it with love and offered it to me because he knew I loved birds.

From very early on until he was a teenager, Micah and I often went bird-watching in the forest or by a lake. When he was very young, he liked to borrow daddy's binoculars. I felt genuine delight in sharing with my beloved child the treasures of nature. He would ask a thousand questions, and, as he grew older, his questions turned into a thousand jokes. It was always a pleasure for me and for others to be in his company. He overflowed with love of life.

A sea of memories flood my mind.

I still see my four children and their mother with whom I shared twenty years of my life. Once more I feel the hurt caused by our divorce. A painful divorce, a brutal rupture, a violent tearing. We were very young, teenagers in fact, when we started our life together. We entered into it like an adventure. We had very good moments and from our union four beautiful children were born.

I can still see myself holding our firstborn in my arms. He has dark skin, black eyes and a small flat nose. He looks at me crying. Then our daughters were born, all cute little darlings. Each time they looked at me, my heart was won over.

I can still feel the warmth of little Micah, sleeping on my chest on this beautiful summer afternoon. I watch him sleep, thinking of the thousand projects and dreams we will accomplish together.

I recall the small hands of my daughters firmly holding my finger as they courageously took their first steps. I see the four of them running after supper from the living room to the kitchen and back, as if unable to contain their energy. I see them running in the grass with their friends, I see them running to me as I'm coming back from work, hugging me tightly with their little arms and climbing on my back for a horseback ride.

121

I see them at the seaside, running in the waves, water splashing everywhere. I see them sitting with me on a small boat, peacefully gliding on a lake...

But one day, water started leaking into this little boat that was our marriage. Despite our efforts, their mother and I were unable to repair the breach. Then the boat hit the rocks, and we were shipwrecked. The children and their mother held onto the wreckage and I, alone, was washed up on an island.

I was the captain, never wishing for such a disaster to happen, but it was impossible to avoid the tragedy. I hated myself; I hated my lack of foresight. I hated my nauseating selfishness.

Our divorce adversely affected my relationship with my children, and particularly with Micah, who no longer wanted to talk to me. His open wounds and his adolescent anger closed all doors. I tried to restore our friendship: I asked forgiveness, I kept sending him letters, little gifts, I even gave him my favourite guitar ...but nothing changed, the door of his heart remained bolted.

And I too sank into a black hole. Health problems started to appear. I lost all motivation and even if I sometimes succeeded in doing some work, I couldn't climb out of my despair. It was only little by little, and with God's help, that it was possible to come out of the fog of confusion and shame. My relationship with my daughters was gradually restored. As for Micah, he was getting worse. His relationship with his mother deteriorated to the point where he had to be placed in foster homes.

I see myself again, scanning the streets and districts of the city, hoping to stumble upon the place where he lived. I suffered deeply from his absence. Sometimes the agony was impossible to tolerate. I sometimes walked the streets, crying, and praying to God that he would at least allow me a glimpse of him, even for a short moment. But it never happened. Maybe I was being prepared for an absence that would last much longer!

After this period, Micah went to live with his grandparents, and stayed with them an entire year. Upon his return to

Quebec, he came in contact with a few young men who were dealing and using drugs, and he continued his descent into despair. Even if Micah's kindness and his deep love for his mother and sisters remained intact, his thoughts grew darker …until that fateful day.

I see myself again beside my dying son and I feel as if my heart will explode. His face is turned toward me, and his eyes are about to close. A tear runs down his cheek …I caress his forehead, his hair. I want to die with him. I am mute, but every cell of my being screams, I LOVE YOU, MICAH!

I gently put my hand on his head and ask God to restore my child's health. More than anything in the world, I wish that God would give us a second chance. But slowly, my hope melts away, and I find myself praying that his peace and his forgiveness would pour over us. I felt a strong sense of heaven's peace come and cover my son, and shortly after this his heart stopped. On that dreadful day, part of my heart, his mother's heart, and the hearts of his three sisters, stopped beating. This unique person, our beautiful Micah whom we loved so much, in the good times and the bad, had left us, closing the door behind him forever.

Had he really intended to leave like this, for good? I don't know …I don't believe so! He wanted to yell, to scream very loud …and he did scream loud, so loud that his cry tore our hearts like paper, like a letter left unfinished. His scream pierced my spirit, driving me crazy …crazy for him.

Micah! My beautiful Micah! I will never forget you.

→>><<←

I am sitting in silence in this basement, and I cannot tear myself away from the little bird feeder, deeply distressed by the ebb and flow of all those pictures from the past flooding my mind. This gift from Micah, this little bird feeder, was a testimony to the love he once felt toward me; a precious love that was deeply rooted in his heart. And it was a love I wasn't always worthy of.

Though imprisoned in the cage of my adult preoccupations, blinded by a multitude of commitments which seemed more and more cumbersome, I had certainly appreciated this little gift Micah offered me. And I had taken the time to put my arms around him and hug and kiss him, and thank him. But the little feeder was never put to use. I must have displayed it for a while before moving it unto a shelf, and then into a box of other "precious" objects I wanted to keep.

I wonder how many more of those "precious" objects found their way onto the shelves of my heart, their beauty eventually covered by the dust of my carelessness and worries? How many broken promises and forgotten dreams are hidden in the drawers of my life and of my children's lives? How many missed opportunities have I collected along my path as a parent? There are many, too many. There are enough for me to hear my name when I look at the figure of the man with a heart of stone in Micah's drawing. There are too many and I cannot change it. The mere thought of not responding properly to the love that my daughters pour on me literally paralyses me. The fear of disappointing them, of hurting them. A fear that has already pushed me into a black hole!

Micah's drawing is for me a thorn in the heart. It forces me to see things as they really are. It helps me to hate my mediocrity and recognize my imperfections. It helps me to ask forgiveness. It inspires me to change the course of my actions. It encourages me to be humble enough to seek help when my own resources fail, when the burdens become too heavy.

I have come to understand for certain things in my life that only God can bring deep transformation and gradually break through the layer of rock covering the true inner beauty of my being. I also understood that this change is never instantaneous and I must accept the fact that love will only shine in me to the degree that I trust him and give him the right to carry my burdens for me. Only love liberates. And I want this freedom to be my banner. I want to be transparent and open in all my relationships. I want to be able to really appreciate the beauty of the treasures in the lives of the people around me and in my children's lives. The rest of my life must be dedicated to enjoying the simple things and focusing on what is really important: loving God and loving others.

This pretty flower Micah painted for me, I now find exceptional. It is the mirror of his soul. More than ever, I savour its fragrance, like that of no other flower on earth. I breathe it in with all my senses.

The little bird feeder is now on my balcony, in full view, so that all the birds in the sky can admire it and come to feed.

Would you know my name
if I saw you in heaven?
Would you feel the same
if I saw you in heaven?
I must be strong and carry on
'Cause I know I don't belong
here in heaven...

Would you hold my hand
if I saw you in heaven?
Would you help me stand
if I saw you in heaven?
I'll find my way through night and day
'Cause I know I just can't stay
here in heaven...

Time can bring you down,
time can bend your knees
Time can break your heart,
have you begging please...

Beyond the door there's peace I'm sure
And I know there'll be no more
tears in heaven...

ERIC CLAPTON & WILL JENNINGS
(Album: Unplugged)

A SONG IN THE NIGHT

YESTERDAY EVENING, THE MAGNIFICENT colours stretching across the skies offered the most glorious of sights. The rose and saffron, the different shades of purple, the lighter blue spilling out from behind the gold of the clouds, all reflecting in the far distance on the silvery crests of the open sea. I stayed there for a long time, sitting on a large weathered stump, probably washed up on this beach many years ago. I felt like a millionaire, sitting on the balcony of a vast amphitheater, the lone spectator, honoured to behold this grandiose presentation bearing the signature of the Creator.

But today, there is fog everywhere. I can hardly distinguish the huge boulders at the opposite end of the beach. The bushes and the flowers that have so often welcomed me here are hidden under an opaque mist. It is impossible to notice the rocky peaks that challenge the fury of the waves as they beat against their base. They are like bulls charging the red flag of a toreador. Invisible also is the small island, which, like a faithful friend, came daily to assure me with its tranquil presence.

Today, everything is white and grey. The waves crash on the shore with unusual force. Their whisper has turned into a roar like that of a lion declaring his domain. Their crests roll in the distance. They strike the beach hard, creating an atmosphere which makes one feel small and vulnerable. Today, the sea rules.

And inside, my soul is fearful. Again I have to face this man with a heart of stone that Micah drew, and my soul cries.

It feels as though a thick fog is hiding the light of my spirit. A fog of rejection, of remorse, and of this heavy guilt that constantly assails me.

I look at this gaunt, lonely man, whose traits display coldness and indifference. I look at him, and I hate him. I hold him responsible for the death of my son. Maybe he could have helped him, but he did not. He is motionless, passive before the sufferings of the wounded one. What a tragedy! He refuses to listen to the traveller asking for the directions, shelter, and water that are necessary to give him the strength he needs to pursue his journey. The man with a heart of stone is of no help.

How long will this man dominate my life? How can he be silenced? How can I again find the joy that once inhabited me?

The worst part is that the fog of my mourning keeps me from seeing clearly how deep this silent character has rooted himself in my life. How well did Micah perceive the truth? How much has this character whom I call 'the man with a heart of stone', influenced the destinies of my son and me?

There are moments when a fragrant breeze blows on my spirit and briefly repels this oppressive fog. The warm light of the sun then restores the true colours to the landscape. It is in these times of lucidity that I am able to clearly see my mistakes and responsibilities as a father. In these blessed moments I can accept objectively, without crumbling under a yoke of condemnation, my failure and ineptitude in building this bond between Micah and me which would have become a strong anchor in the raging storms. Of course, this bond once existed between us, but over the years it broke, and Micah's boat drifted away, until the waves of adversity hurled it against the rocks.

These gentle breezes, those moments of respite, allowed me to preserve the hope that better days would come, hope that my suffering would end and that God had not abandoned me.

Then, one night, while listening to the words of a song by Marie-Denise Pelletier, I cried. Though I didn't really understand what was happening, it seemed that this song had a particular message for me. I had heard it before, but never really paid attention to the lyrics or allowed them to reach inside me.

Like a fool throws to the sea
Empty bottles filled with hopes
Someone will read through the glass
My S.O.S. written with my breath
Telling you I'm lonely
Sketching a desert without ink

And I run, grabbing hold of life again
Drunk with the sound
Of bodies around me
Branches woven in braids
Oblivious to the distress
Of the words I send

It is hard to call for help
When so many tragedies oppress
And tears tied in knots of stress
Choke the cries of love
Of those heavy in weakness
With their last hope vanishing

And I run, grabbing hold of life again
Drunk with the sound
Of bodies around me
Branches woven in braids
Oblivious to the distress
Of the words I send

All the cries, the S.O.S.
Vanish in the air, the water only bears their trace
Beauty in the breaking of the waves
Prisoners of glass vessels
Letters try to sail but the waves bring them back
Stars of glass bursting on the rocks

129

I picked up the broken glass
Rebuilding the whole picture
It was clear as crystal
Can't do anything against the past
Heroes would have to be replaced
In a world where harmony still awaits.

And as the music gradually engulfed my whole being, it was as if a veil were being removed. I felt my spirit burst with illumination as divine light enveloped me. Like pieces of a puzzle, the words of the song came to life before my eyes.

The fool, in the song, is me. I am this fool that keeps throwing empty bottles into the sea, bottles containing the ghosts of my past failures. I keep being conquered by the death that has conquered my son. I refuse to accept that I am still part of a world where the most beautiful things remain to be done, even if the scar left by Micah's departure will always remain on my heart.

I had been unaware that the image of this man with a heart of stone had become a greater burden than the suffering of my loss. Yes! Micah did hurt! Yes! I could have been a better father! Yes! I have to accept my part of the responsibility for this tragedy! But the ghost I am now carrying on my shoulders has become heavier than the wounded one in the drawing. Finally, it is my own distress that I carry; it is my own death. I crumble. I become worn out under my own burden. And this could be the end of me!

It is said that in ancient Rome, to punish a murderer, they would bind the body of his victim to him until its rotting flesh actually transferred to the murderer's body. But here, it is not the corpse of my own son that is on me; it is the weight of my own guilt!

Finally, I see light piercing the darkness in my life. I see an opening in the clouds. The fog is being pushed back by the emerging light of the sun. I feel it ...the sky will finally clear, the sun will appear.

I often go and spend a few hours in the library, without briefcase or computer. I walk down the aisles nonchalantly, taking time to open books that attract my attention. I don't know much about the history of art, but I take great pleasure in browsing through those large books containing the works of the great masters.

During one such visit I discovered a painting that particularly sparked my interest, a painting by Rembrandt entitled *The Return of the Prodigal Son*. It illustrates the Biblical parable of the father who, having waited for a long time for the return of his younger son, finally sees him coming back and runs to welcome him with open arms. The painting shows the son, bald, in rags, his head resting on the chest of his father, whose face expresses tenderness and compassion. In this work the artist portrayed much more than a simple illustration of a text from the Bible. He expressed the beauty of forgiveness that resides in the heart of God.

History reveals that the life of that painter had not been exempt from struggles and reckless living. At the time of the creation of this masterpiece, Rembrandt had reached maturity, and what he put on the canvas was his own soul. A soul that had suffered and was now turning to God to taste of his love and his healing. In effect, during the sixty-three years of his life, Rembrandt witnessed the death not only of his wife, Saskia, but also of three sons, two daughters, and two more wives. In his memoirs he didn't address the pain he felt at the death of his beloved son, Titus, but the character of the father in *The Prodigal Son* certainly suggests the tears it cost him.

In his excellent book, *The Return of the Prodigal Son*, Henri Nouwen, former professor at Harvard University, offers detailed comments on this painting that has become for him a window into eternity. The impact this painting had on his life brought him into a new dimension of God's love and forgiveness, which he later communicated in the Ark Communities where he spent many years working with mentally-handicapped people. He writes:

"The father's hands are at the heart of this painting by Rembrandt. It is on the hands that all the light is focused; it is to them that the eyes are drawn. In these hands, we see mercy incarnate. Through them, forgiveness, reconciliation and healing operate, through which, in turn, not only the tired son but also the exhausted father find rest."

What a marvellous truth and how I need to see it at work in my life! Only God's love and forgiveness can bring healing to the hearts of sons and fathers. Only his love is able to help me forgive Micah for leaving us so brutally and also to forgive myself. Only God's love can help me overcome my weaknesses. God is not a human father, imperfect. His fatherly love is rich enough and strong enough to embrace each of his sons and daughters equally. Doctor Serge Chaussé, in my book-compilation of doctors' testimonies, expresses it this way: "God is my Father. I do not think that he will beat me if I do something wrong. On the contrary, I believe he will cry. He will be sad over the fix I got myself into. He will not say, *'I told you so. Tough luck. Next time, you'll just have to listen to me.'* Only our earthly fathers think that way. As far as I am concerned, God is different."

His love excludes no one. It reaches into the deepest abyss to remind us that we are not alone; God, our Father, is with us wherever we are, and he shares our suffering. And this, he proved to me at a time in my life when I thought all was lost. Healing is slow, and the changes I would like to see in my life don't simply happen at the snap of a finger. But God renewed both my hope and zest for life. I'm privileged to enjoy happy times with my three beautiful daughters whom I love so much. I am surrounded by my family, by a wife who loves me, and by good friends. And even if the scar caused by Micah's departure remains on my soul, I have to stay open to the work of God's love in my life.

After reading a few stories from Rembrandt's life, I wondered what life was like during his era. Could Rembrandt and Saskia's roles as parents be compared to those of today? What were their worries and preoccupations? How many nights did they stay up thinking about the learning disabilities of their young son, the terrible headaches of their younger daughter, or the grief of their older daughter after her fiancé called off the engagement? Were their children's needs for affection fulfilled in their household? What about those of the father and the mother? How about other families during that time? Did parents succeed in maintaining harmony between their children and those in the neighbourhood? Were the children of that time more obedient or more rebellious, more tender or more hardhearted? What did they do for amusement? What were their hopes and dreams?

Thinking about people's lives in those times, I don't believe their struggles are different from ours. Certainly the Dutch culture and customs of the seventeenth century cannot be compared to our modern way of life, but aren't human beings basically the same, no matter where they live, when they live, or what their customs are?

Personally, I believe that throughout history there have been good and bad people, good and not so good parents, that families always faced issues of poverty, conflict, adultery, sickness, death, and a multitude of unexpected and uncontrollable situations, similar to those we face today. Family life improves the existence of some individuals, while others experience it as a source of anguish and bitterness. It has always been the case. For still others, the terrible struggles they had to go through in their childhood will inexplicably be transformed into a grand symphony, as was the case with young Ludwig van Beethoven, whose music exudes a depth of emotion and power of expression that is without equal.

Going even further back in history, we have to admit that family life was never exempt from difficulties. The first family mentioned in the Bible, Adam and Eve's, was torn apart by terrible tragedy: the death of their son Abel, killed by Cain, his own brother. Later, Lot's daughters made him drink until he fell asleep so they could take turns and commit incest with him. Then, Abraham, whose affair with a servant gave rise to serious family conflicts. And later Jacob, his grandson, from whom the Israelites descended, was polygamous. King David, a sensitive man who loved God passionately, had his share of dark moments. He committed adultery with the wife of a deeply loyal man and then had him murdered. The child born from this illicit union died. Later, another of David's sons, Absalom, rebelled against his father with violence. Another son, Solomon, had a very confused family life, even as he penned the most beautiful romantic poem of all times: *The Song of Songs*.

Clearly, God never asked the Biblical writers to hide the mistakes and failures of the great figures of ancient times. This can help us understand why Jesus and the writers of the New Testament give family life and sexual purity such a key role. God is touched by all true repentance from the heart of man and his forgiveness is infinite. However, harmonious family relationships where love reigns and where each member can develop in a healthy environment are held high in God's esteem.

I therefore felt very guilty toward God for not being able to keep my family together. I was even jealous of friends' families who lived in harmony. The loss of my job, our house, and the financial difficulties that followed did nothing, of course, to lighten my sense of guilt.

Nevertheless, I know now that nothing is impossible for God. I know that he loves me unconditionally and that with him, it is possible to rebuild a life and know better days. Isn't that the blessing of his forgiveness?

It was by integrating this truth into my life that it became possible for me to appreciate other people's successes without always feeling inferior or condemned. I can now appreciate the things that are beautiful about my own life and my own personality. I can also appreciate beauty in the lives of others, beauty I once could not see, though it existed around me. I also believe that I now can better understand certain aspects of life.

An example in question occurred some time ago when I visited my family in Hébertville. My sister Rachel and her husband André were married when I was a toddler. On the day of the wedding, Rachel was a real princess in a white dress with a crinoline, light as a ballerina. Everyone in the family knew that her fiancé, André, would be a good husband.

Soon after their marriage their first child was born, a beautiful and healthy boy they called Martin. His parents were delighted. Months went by and gradually Rachel and André noticed a number of abnormalities in their son's growth and development. They consulted their family doctor and specialists who found that there was definitely something wrong. Martin showed signs of cerebral palsy. His mouth wasn't developing normally, and he had to undergo a series of operations. His eyesight was poor and he was forced to wear glasses with thick lenses.

Saddened, the parents had to face the reality that Martin would never be like other children. He wouldn't go to school like the others, could never be part of a ball team or play hockey. At times he would be rejected, ridiculed by his peers, and could not adequately express his emotions, his sorrows, and his hurts.

Years have passed, and the doctors' diagnosis proved to be true. Martin took a long time to learn how to walk, eat, and accomplish tasks other children learn instinctively. He started uttering nasal sounds, and little by little he was able to pronounce syllables and words. The difficulties associated with his growth were a challenge for Rachel and André, but they faced this challenge with patience and love.

With the help of organizations specializing in educating people with mental handicaps, Martin achieved a considerable level of independence. He developed his artistic talents through discovering colours and shapes. He also developed his physical abilities so that he was part of a hockey team for handicapped people. He can ride a big tricycle adapted to his motor skills, and he goes shopping on his own for small items. He has held jobs in a nail factory, on a farm, and he currently works in a small boutique called *The Faithful Friend,* specializing in pet care. His wages are minimal, but Martin is happy to work. His employers say that he is a model employee. All those who spend time with him appreciate him because he radiates happiness and joy. He is truly for one and all a "faithful friend," without prejudice or malice.

Martin is a ray of sunshine for our family. Every day after work he visits my mother and brings her the newspaper or treats of some kind. When I go to Hébertville and find myself in his presence, this contagious joy that he exudes literally floods me. Martin's life continually speaks to me and inspires me to become a better person, more agreeable and friendlier with others. If only I could love people like Martin loves them, I too would be a bearer of happiness. Having Martin as my nephew is a great privilege, even if I have not always responded to him in kind.

I believe he wears his name magnificently: Martin Lajoie. "Lajoie" literally means, "joy".

❧

Some time ago, I was told the most moving story. It was that of a severely handicapped child and his father whose life had been completely transformed by a dream he will never forget.

In the dream, the father is in heaven with Jesus, with the angels, and with other people he doesn't recognize. The atmosphere of this place is absolutely indescribable. The flow of life there can be literally felt, so purely, even as the clearest crystal. The quality of love can be compared to music never before heard on earth. There is a lot of activity, but everything flows in absolute peace.

The man approaches a group of young people of great beauty, gathered as if in a classroom. In front of them stands a young man even more perfect in beauty and wisdom. When this young man speaks, his whole audience listens intently, captivated by all of his words. His incomparable knowledge elicits approving comments, even at times exclamations of admiration.

Dazzled by this moving scene, the father slowly comes closer to hear the words of this young man who has the appearance of an angel. As he approaches, he feels his heart

136

leap with intense love for this one he now begins to recognize. The face strikes him as familiar. And those eyes. He has met them so many times before. It's the gaze of his young handicapped son! Hard to believe, but it is him. This child, who had been deprived of language and knowledge during his sojourn on earth, had now received infinite wisdom, which he could share freely for all eternity.

Though this was only a dream, it is one that could conceivably become reality some day. And why not? Is it not like God to elevate the humble, the little ones, the destitute? Wasn't the King of Kings born in a stable among poor shepherds? Hasn't Jesus promised heavenly rewards to those who are poor in spirit?

After this dream, the father of the young handicapped child never looked at his son the same way. A window had opened on a heavenly reality he had never seen before. Through this window, he could see beyond the handicap of his child, the atrophied limbs, and his difficulty communicating. He saw his son in perfect health, in the realm of eternal glory.

To believe in the existence of heaven or of life after death, as Jesus taught, requires faith. But since there were those who reported that the Resurrected One appeared before a crowd of witnesses, and they transmitted this notion of a hereafter to us, it is possible for it to be true. And for those who believe in Christ, this truth is essential. The true Christian does not perceive his earthly life as a painful waiting ordeal, filled with insecurity, as he awaits the day he will plead his case before God at the heavenly Supreme Court. In fact, if it were so, no one would win his case. Because no one can ever be good enough to gain access to Paradise.

Nobody on earth can "pay his way" to heaven. The price is much too high. Only God can grant a person the privilege of living with him for eternity. And this he already accomplished by coming among us, by bearing the guilt of our sins and freeing us from condemnation. Jesus died on the cross to demonstrate the extremes of human wickedness and the grace of God.

Heaven therefore starts here as we establish friendship with God. It is this friendship and not our competence in spiritual matters that will continue on after death, for eternity. Doesn't the Bible say that the one who loves Jesus in this life will be loved by him in the next? That's heaven! A love story that even death cannot destroy. It is up to us to take time to consider the words of Christ and invite him to be our friend. He never refuses such an invitation!

For those parents who have to experience the death of a child, the hope of some day seeing the one they love again can become a source of enduring comfort. This reality doesn't cancel out the sadness caused by the departure of that child, but it does provide strength that will carry them through their season of grief.

⇢⇠

After the births of my first two children, I lived several years in the city of Repentigny, a suburb of Montreal. I have a treasure of unforgettable memories from this time. I had some beautiful, sincere friendships. Other memories are more painful, but sincere friendships are not forged in happy times only; they can also be developed in times of sadness.

When I first met Helene, I immediately felt that she was shy and extremely sensitive. The slightest remark concerning her made her blush. Her great sensitivity, though, made her quickly become an excellent friend. She also became part of our family. Helene suffered from a slight mental handicap that made her a bit slow at learning certain tasks. But often this slight handicap, together with her unique sense of humour, made her all the more endearing. She lived with us for several months in a little room we built for her. Helene was a true friend to our whole family.

One day, I went out with a group of teenagers to a restaurant in Montreal. Helene was with us. After the meal, we had planned to go to the Olympic stadium pool for a swim. During the meal Helene felt ill. She went to the bathroom with a friend, but her condition got steadily worse. She suffered from asthma, and sometimes, when her breathing was too erratic, I would go to the hospital with her so she could receive treatment. So I suggested we go to the hospital, only a few minutes from the restaurant. She preferred to wait, feeling that her breathing was not too bad, and would stabilize on its own. So we left for the swimming pool. On the way, her condition rapidly deteriorated, much more quickly than was normal for an asthma attack, and too quickly for us to make it to the hospital on time. We were unaware of the fact that Helene had suffered from an allergic reaction to the peanut oil-based salad dressing which she had eaten during the meal. Her allergic reaction proved fatal.

On this beautiful sunny afternoon, Helene left us suddenly for her heavenly dwelling. It was a terrible shock for her parents who adored her. What grief for the members of her family and her numerous friends to see this little dove fly away without even being able to say good-bye! Why do such tragedies happen? And why Helene? Many questions remain unanswered. All I know is that if we truly believe in God and eternity, it is more than likely that some of those answers will be given to us in the hereafter.

I think of another friend, younger than Helene, but who also left us through equally tragic circumstances.

On the front page of the *Journal de Montréal*, October 23, 1999, we could read in big letters: STOP SIGN IGNORED, TEENAGER HIT. ALCOHOL KILLS! With the article was a full-sized picture of Mylène, brimming with life, her authentic smile and her teasing eyes sending one last goodbye to all who loved her.

Fifteen happy years …and suddenly, it's all over. A drunk driver, a repeat offender, runs through a stop sign, and hits Mylène, throwing her into the air.

Neither Gilles and Manon Carignan, her parents, nor Anissa and Noémie, her two sisters, could ever have imagined that Mylène would leave them in such an unexpected way, and under such tragic circumstances.

I had known the Carignan family for many years. They are my friends. Mylène was my friend, too, and her departure broke my heart. A few hours after the accident, I joined them at the hospital by Mylène's bedside where she lay motionless. It was hard to recognize her because her face was so puffy. She had already stopped breathing.

For fifteen years, Mylène had been loved and cherished by the most affectionate family I know. A model family in all regards, and this is no exaggeration!

I have been a friend of the Carignans for years. My children played with theirs, and with Mylène. Seeing her picture next to that of a drunk driver, on the front page, stirred in me such indignation, repulsion, and anger! This man had no right to steal a life because of his alcohol addiction. And especially in the case of Mylène, such a unique, irreplaceable person. Her friends at school called her "sunshine" for her genuine interest in others, and her optimism. Her love of life was a halo that shone and touched everyone around.

She had the talent of an artist, and was always available as a confidante.

The night before her accident, Mylène took part in a youth meeting during which each one was asked to write a short text, as if it were a letter written by God, communicating his love to a friend. This letter was then to be given to someone randomly picked by the meeting facilitator. By pure "coincidence", Mylène's letter ended up in her sister Anissa's hands. And this is what she wrote:

> *"My dear child, You are the apple of my eye, the girl I have fashioned, from heaven, with love and care. In your days of sorrows, when times were hard, I was there to comfort you. I would raise mountains to rescue you. O how I love you… I died on the Cross for you. I am longing for that day when you will come and be with me, in my most holy place…*
>
> *Your loving Father… (Mylène)*

I believe that message was directly inspired by God, not only for Anissa, but also, in a certain way, for Mylène who was to join him the next day in his most holy place!

140

Mylène knew God's love, as her parents and sisters do. And despite the extreme agony and emptiness left by the departure of their beloved Mylène, they turned toward the Source of all comfort to journey through this season of grief. God also is the One who guided them to healing and forgiveness.

Gilles and Manon are good friends. I can still see them beside their daughter's coffin, as though a sword was piercing their hearts. However, I knew that despite the flood of sorrow which was overtaking them, they would let the light and warmth inside them shine all the brighter. I knew that one day, as had often been the case before, the Carignans would become a source of comfort for the hurting, the broken... and the mourning.

And it didn't take long before it happened. In an article published in the November 1999, issue of the magazine *Dernière Heure*, Gilles shares his thoughts regarding the man responsible for the death of their daughter:

"On the spur of the moment, is there any parent who would not harbour anger toward one who has harmed their child? But eventually you ask yourself, should one individual carry all the blame when the whole of society is responsible? How many people do we know who have driven their cars after having had too much to drink? Such people need to be taken care of and helped rather than blamed.

"And forgiving does not mean we are not hoping justice will prevail. God doesn't remove the consequences of one's actions. He does, however, offer the opportunity to those of us who have been wronged to free ourselves from the spirit of condemnation. Forgiveness is not a feeling; it's a choice. Deep down, I do not think this man intended to hurt Mylène. But, even if he had acted intentionally, he would still be just an ordinary human being who made a fatal error in judgement.

"In our family, we distinguish between the sin and the sinner. At the same time, we are not blind: this man deserves a good "spanking", a proper punishment. This sad event has to be enough to help him make definite changes in his life.

141

Human justice alone, however, is not capable of achieving this change.

"There is one state in America where bar owners are severely punished if one of their customers is allowed to drive away drunk and causes an accident. You know, I am the son of an alcoholic. My father used to beat my mother and me… he was a real bother for our neighbours. Then he was placed in a psychiatric ward for 25 years. But my mother taught us to forgive him. Toward the end of his life, he realized the harm he had caused and started to change, radically. It was incredible to witness how my father was transformed after he realized his mistakes.

"We want to meet this man who caused our daughter's death, in a place other than at the inquiry and ensuing trial. We so want to help him. If he had crossed Mylène's path in obvious need, she would have helped him, as she always did. It is also to honour her that we are inviting this man to walk the path of forgiveness with us."

This testimony from Gilles stirs my feelings of love toward him and his family. If Mylène was always ready to help and forgive, it's because she had learned from her parents, who, in turn, had learned from God. Forgiveness is like a gift that God gently sets deeply in our hearts. It is like a river slowly transforming the sharp rocks of bitterness into small, smooth pebbles. Forgiveness cannot count on human strength. Without God's help, all such efforts would be in vain. Forgiveness is a gift we must ask for and receive from God, a gift we then give to people who sometimes are undeserving.

Forgiveness is never deserved; it is received. It is not a burden forced upon us by others or by ourselves. To forgive others for the evil done to us, we have to walk the path of forgiveness daily. And this road is a rocky road, where bitterness, anger, and hate are often our companions. But whatever befalls us, we must keep on walking, step by step, open to God. "I'm unable to forgive this person, but I receive in my heart your love and forgiveness." Over time, God's forgiveness works in us, and his forgiveness becomes ours. It is the most precious gift that can be offered to us and that we can offer to others. Forgiving... for giving!

A few months after the accident, Gilles and Manon met with the man responsible for their daughter's death and expressed their sincere forgiveness to him. This initiative has the potential to radically transform his life.

The light I see shining in the eyes of Gilles, Manon, and their children is the reflection of God's love. A love that is not of this world but that God offers to all who love him and turn to him. This love will never die, neither on earth, nor in the hereafter!

I again look at the sad silhouette of the three characters in Micah's drawing, and I have the impression they still have something to tell me. The man with a heart of stone looks even skinnier, the traveller more worried, and the wounded one seems to groan with even more intensity.

I keep silent. I watch. I listen. I try to better understand human suffering... my son's sufferings. Then a window opens. I watch, and now I see. I see the wounded one and the traveller, back to back. Micah's sketch portrays a duality, a schism — a breach between heart and reason, strength and weakness, good and evil. This duality created doubt and confusion in Micah's life. A tearing between heart and reason that pushed him to his limit, taking him over the edge in an act that could have been more a cry for help. Could it have been a distress call? After all, did not the method he chose to end his suffering leave the possibility that he would survive? And after the act, did he not leave his apartment hoping to find help?

Micah was probably torn between death and life. In his weakness, he wished to put an end to his pain quickly, but in his strength, he wished to live. In his grief, he delivered himself to evil, but it was the good he could feel in himself that he was calling to, with all of his strength. It is his tender heart, his wounded heart, which, unable to listen to reason, pierced the abscess of his wound. A wound that seemed to him to be too serious, too deep... incurable!

I see in this duality the eternal love-pain paradox that is found at the heart of the human journey. This quest for well-being, pleasure and love, which too often turns into disappointment, hurt and hate. It is the tragedy of a divorce, of a broken heart, when after giving the best of what we are, we find ourselves wounded and rejected within it.

It is the negation of love. It is the cry of an entire generation that has suffered the failure of their parents' love story. The cry of a whole generation that sought in vain, through all kinds of experiences, to comfort and restore its ability to love and be loved. Experiences that were really nothing but attempts to silence the echo of their childhood dreams crushed under the rock of disappointment. To try and negate this astonishing paradox that the "perfect love story" does not exist, they offer to the world their most intimate selves, their sexuality.

What they get in return is often far from the feelings of tenderness and authenticity they so long for. Their identity suffers, and their self-esteem has to submit to society's definition of true happiness. They know this happiness is artificial, copied from a Hollywood version that at times portrays their daily reality, and at times their most inaccessible fantasies.

There again, this duality tears at the soul. The noblest feelings of beauty and grandeur dwelling in their spirits constantly crash upon the dissatisfaction generated by a lifestyle geared toward self-gratification. The truth is, true happiness is not found in the quest for pleasure and power. If it were the case, the rich and beautiful young women and those sensual young men, now idolized by thousands of teenagers, would be the happiest people in the world. It is clearly not the case. Whether it is the plaster or bronze statues of ancient civilizations, or the tapestries of pictures taken from tabloids and plastered all over the bedroom walls of North-American youth, these idols never bring tangible help to a world in disarray.

I respect the philanthropic gestures of artists like Madonna who donate huge sums of money for the treatment of people suffering from the AIDS virus. The problem is that Madonna herself promoted the worst of sexual perversions to her fans! What a paradox! May God bless her soul if this is the sign of true repentance!

If only those "new prophets" of the third millennium could grasp the pertinence of the message communicated by certain youth that lived in Biblical times. If they could research and express the beauty of the passionate love that Daniel, Ezekiel and David, for instance, had for God and for his commandments. If they could understand how those young people succeeded in profoundly impacting the conscience of a whole generation. If the artists of the 21st century would turn to God, we would witness the healing of our nation.

And what does God think of all this? Why doesn't he intervene? If he exists, doesn't our degeneration bother him? Can't he do anything about it?

What a contradiction! An all-powerful God who does nothing... who does nothing for me!

This stiff character, cold as the marble of the cathedrals, distant and insensitive to our woes, Micah portrayed well. For him, he personified his own father. A father unable to ease his pain, unable to meet his needs. Looking at the picture, I can hear my son's thoughts: "You are so mean, so mean in your own self-pity... it would have been better if you hadn't been born. That way, my pain would have been lighter than having to endure this image of you which haunts me. But since you were always stronger than I was, it is I who will now win this ultimate battle. I will put an end to the tragedy of my life. I will destroy myself, me, your masterpiece, and you won't be able to stop me."

How my heart bleeds as I write these lines! If only Micah had known how much I loved him. Despite my meanness, my incompetence, my mistakes. I was burned and broken by despair. If only he could have seen in my eyes the sadness, the tenderness and the hope I had for better days with him.

This wretched character to whom the traveller turns could also represent other kinds of people : a depressed spouse, an authoritative mother, a disillusioned girlfriend, a life partner who is alcoholic, an absent parent, a broken friendship, a society unable to help its own wounded, or, maybe even God. A mean god, cold and distant, unwilling to come to the rescue; a nameless god, without personality, out of reach; a god with a thousand faces inflicting a karma on me, to which my destiny is helplessly chained, or an authoritarian god constantly raising the stakes so that whatever I do, I will never meet his expectations. This god is stingy with his love, he cannot help me. I don't know if he really exists. Rather, I think he exists in the heads of some, and I prefer not to be introduced to him. He is an abusive, evil being!

⇒≫≪⇐

I recently met a Protestant pastor who shared his pain and worries regarding one of his children. This pastor's family life was happy and peaceful. When one of his sons reached his teens, he began to show signs of psychological unbalance. One day this son knelt for hours at the foot of his bed, his Bible open before him, pleading with God to come and help him, and free him of his terrible torment. Seeing no immediate result, he got up and ran away from home.

What a shock to the hearts of his parents! They would have loved to take their son in their arms and comfort him. They would gladly have taken upon themselves the heavy burden that afflicted his spirit. They would have suffered in his stead. But, saddened and worried, they had no other choice than to see their love crash upon the thick wall of their son's depression, this prison in which their beloved child was moaning, his feet in shackles.

How did this young man perceive the desperate efforts of his parents in their attempts to rescue him? Did he interpret their reactions as weakness, as harassment? Why did he choose to turn his back and run away? Why didn't God do something? Why didn't he reach out his hand to rescue this child in distress? Is God overwhelmed by the circumstances? Did he remove his presence? Is he like this character portrayed by the skinny silhouette of the man with a heart of stone that Micah drew, cold and powerless?

Is God really like that?

Even if I have to admit that I understand very little of God's personality, I am convinced that God is Love. He chose to be born in the midst of a weak and conquered nation, in a stable located in a tiny town. He came to the poor, the workers and the farmers. He could not limit himself to communicating with us from a distance, but he took human form to convince us that he truly loved us.

To tell the truth, the face of God greatly resembles that of Jesus. He is tanned by the sun and covered with dust from the country roads where he walked to bring the Bread of Life to people... the words of life eternal. The face of God is wrinkled. We can read from the lines on his face that long hours were spent listening to and healing the destitute, the poor, the orphans, and the widows.

His face displays a tender smile, a childlike smile, like that of the children that ran to meet him at the entrances of villages, dancing and singing. And Jesus danced and sang with them.

His face is sometimes filled with tenderness and mercy. Simon Peter witnessed it after publicly denying him three times. Jesus then turned around and looked at him affectionately.

We see his face shine in each tear that runs down his cheeks as he is dying on the cross and cries out, "Father, forgive them for they don't know what they're doing!"

But now, his face radiates with incomparable brightness, more brilliant than the sun in all its splendour. This same brightness illuminated the tomb on Easter morning, where neither death nor the powers of darkness could hold him captive. It is the light of the glory of God that his disciples witnessed on the Mount of Transfiguration.

And even if our problems are not always resolved instantly down here, God is with us in our sufferings and our difficulties. He promised that if we kept our faith in him, we would one day see his face.

-->><<<-

The son of my pastor friend is still battling with the terrible scourge of mental illness. I pray to God with all my strength that he will sustain these parents and this family in their difficult trial, and especially that he will protect and heal their cherished son. I pray for the doctors who treat him and I ask God to crown their efforts with success.

147

One more prayer before obeying
The order of the day
and the way of our fathers
Before leaving

One more life saved from oblivion
Carved deeper than with a blade
In the memory of Abraham

Hours of waiting
Heavy grief in our hearts
But greater is our love and faith in you
Even though your thoughts
are so out of our reach

What destinies await us from afar
A little peace, love, and daily bread
In the palm of your hands

Hours of waiting
Heavy grief in our hearts
But greater is our love and faith in you
Even though your thoughts
are so out of our reach

Lead our children till the end of time
Filled with more happiness than sorrows
In the memory of Abraham.

CELINE DION
(Album: D'eux)

THE TITANIC

SUNDAY, APRIL 14, 1912. The weather is cool and the sea is calm. The stars sparkle in a clear sky, playfully reflecting their beauty on the quiet waters of the Atlantic Ocean. Off the coast of Nova Scotia, a gigantic ocean liner glides on the icy waters, at a speed of twenty-two knots. From the shore, all we can see are thousands of little fires advancing in the night, like the Milky Way adorning the heavens. One could mistake it for a town in the midst of a celebration. The ship's smoke-stacks reach for the heavens like the towers of an invincible fortress.

The R.M.S. Titanic is the technological masterpiece of the dawn of the twentieth century and the pride of England. Besides passengers, it carries mail under the auspices of His Majesty King George V. The dimensions of the ship are unprecedented. It measures 882.5 feet long by 95 feet wide. Its height, from keel to smokestack, is 173 feet; its weight, 52,250 tons. By themselves, the three propellers weigh 98 tons. There were 29 boilers in the hold and 12 storage-rooms containing 17,000 cubic yards of coal. The number of rivets in the hull reached 3 million.

The ship can hold 2,603 passengers: 905 in first class, 564 in second, and 1,134 in third. The crew is made up of 900 people. The ship is equipped with 20 lifeboats, the number of which, however, can only accommodate 1,178 people.

The price of a first class cabin with three or four servants is $4,500.00. A bunk bed in third class is $40.00. During this voyage, the safe contained in excess of $300 million worth of jewels (including a chest of diamonds belonging to a mining company from South Africa, the copy of a 12th century Persian manuscript, the Rubiyat of the poet Omar Khayyam, the cover of which was adorned with 1,050 precious stones).

The value of the ship in the currency of that day was $7.5 million. One of the women passengers described it as a floating city. "Just like a city; we lack nothing". There was a swimming pool, a concert hall, and libraries. With all its boutiques and attractions, the main deck was larger than the main street of the city she came from.

The Titanic left Southampton, England, for New York. Many high society people were on board. Charlotte Drake Martinez Cardeza, billionaire wife of the Philadelphia state prosecutor and the daughter of Thomas Drake, banker and industrialist. She occupied one of the first class luxury suites with a private walkway. Colonel John Jacob Astor, also a billionaire and owner of the Astoria and Waldorf hotels in New York. Benjamin Guggenheim, nicknamed "the copper king," a great art collector, born to a rich family of mine and foundry owners. Luigi Gatti, a young Italian, owner of two restaurants in London and manager of the À la Carte restaurant on board the Titanic. Charles Melville Hays, the "railroad king," general director of the Grand Trunk Pacific Railway, a Canadian railroad company. Also among the passengers was Margaret Brown, one of the first American women to run for public office and who was elected to the Senate eight years before women obtained the right to vote.

Two other passengers were directly involved in the saga of the Titanic: Edward John Smith, the ship's captain, as well as Joseph Bruce Ismay, the president of the White Star Line. Ismay was in the habit of joining the maiden voyages of his ships, and the Titanic's was not an exception. He was the one occupying the other first class luxury suite.

Ismay bragged profusely about the features of the Titanic and organized a huge advertising campaign to promote this first voyage, a campaign that boasted, among other things, that "even God would be unable to sink this ship". During the trip, it was he who pushed Captain Smith to increase the speed of the ship despite the risk of hitting an iceberg. And we know what happened as a result!

In spite of the numerous warning messages intercepted by Jack Phillips, the radio dispatcher, the captain refused to slow down. Frederick Fleet, from his vantagepoint in the crow's nest, was the first to spot the iceberg. He later revealed that he didn't have binoculars in the crow's nest, and that if he had, he could have spotted the iceberg from two to two and a half miles away, which would have given them time to steer away from the iceberg.

What a tragedy! This accident could easily have been avoided.

One of the passengers of the Titanic, the young Jack Thayer, seventeen at the time, tells us in his own words what happened next:

"My father had gone to bed, and my mother and I were about to do the same. There was no big impact; I was standing at the time and I don't think it was enough to even make a person lose his balance. I immediately threw on my overcoat and quickly rushed to deck A on the portside. I saw nothing. I headed for the stern to see if there was any trace of ice. The only ice I saw was on the deck. I couldn't see very far ahead of me because I had just come from a brightly-lit room.

I went back down to our cabin and, with my father and mother, made my way to deck A on the starboard side. We saw nothing. My father thought he saw little chunks of ice floating on the water, but I couldn't see anything. There was no big iceberg. We went to the portside and then the ship listed on that side. We stayed there staring into the night for about five minutes. The listing increased very slowly.

We went back down to our cabins on deck C and rushed to put on all our clothes. We all got our lifejackets on and put our coats on over them. We then hurried back to the deck looking everywhere until women were ordered to assemble on the portside.

My father and I said farewell to my mother at the top of the stairs of deck A. Along with her maid, she went directly to deck A on the portside and we proceeded to the starboard side. At that point we had no idea that the ship would sink, and we walked along deck A and then went down to deck B. We met the 1st Steward of the ship's great lounge, who informed us that my mother hadn't yet boarded a lifeboat and he took us to her.

My father and mother were walking ahead of me, and I followed. They went down to deck B and I faced a crowd that cut me off from them. I lost sight of them. As soon as I could make my way through the crowd, I looked for them on deck B, but without success. It was the last time I saw my father.

It was about half an hour later that the ship sank. I went to the starboard side, thinking that my father and mother were aboard a lifeboat. At that time I was accompanied by a friend named Milton C. Long, from New York, whom I had just met that night.

The lifeboats left quickly from the starboard side. Some were already so far out in the water that they could no longer be seen from the ship. We thought we could find room in the last one from the head of the ship, but there seemed to be such a crowd that I thought it wouldn't be safe to try to board it. Milton and I were beside the bow of one of the boats that had just left. I could see no one I knew except Mr. Lingley whom I had also just met that evening. I lost sight of him in just a few minutes. Long and I were near the rail a short distance from the captain's bridge.

The listing on the port side kept increasing. At that point, people started to jump from the stern. I thought of doing the same thing, but I was afraid I would be knocked unconscious on hitting the water. Three times I made up my mind to let myself down by the rope hanging from the bow and try to swim out to one of the lifeboats already at a distance from the ship, but each time Long pulled me back and told me to wait a moment. He then sat down and I stayed standing, waiting for what was to come. Even then we thought it was possible for the ship to stay afloat.

I then saw a rope between the bows as well as a star and I realized it was slowly disappearing. At that moment, the ship lifted, balanced, and then began sinking quite rapidly at an angle of about 30 degrees. As the ship went down, we left the bows and returned to the rail, about half way from the second smokestack.

Long and I said good-bye and we jumped onto the rail. He placed his legs on the other side, waited a minute, and asked me if I was coming. I answered that I was coming in a minute. He never really jumped but slid along the ship. I never saw him again. About five seconds later, I jumped, feet first. I was a good distance from the ship; I fell into the water and as I came back up, something pushed me away from the ship.

The ship seemed surrounded by a bright glow and appeared against the night to be in flames. Water was licking the base of the first smokestack. On board, a crowd of people were rushing toward the back, always toward the back, trying to reach the stern that was still above water. The uproar and the screams continued, punctuated by the explosions and the tearing of the boilers and the machines as they were ripped from their bases.

Suddenly, the whole superstructure of the ship seemed to break in two, a clean break in the front, with one part lying flat and the other rising to the sky. The second smokestack, wide enough for two cars to pass side by side in it, tore from its base with a flash of sparks. I thought it would collapse on me, and in fact it missed me by about 10 yards. The suction it caused pulled me underwater and I had to struggle to make my way back up, completely exhausted.

At that point, I was once more pulled downward and, as I came back up, was again pushed and twisted by a huge wave, rising amidst a vast amount of small debris. Removing my hand from my head, I touched the cork on the side of a life raft that had returned (raft B). Looking up, I saw a few men on board and asked them to lift me out of the water. One of them, a chauffeur, helped me aboard. Soon the bottom of the raft contained thirty to thirty-five men. As I embarked, I was facing the ship.

The decks of the ship were turned slightly toward us. We could see the crowd of about 1,500 people still onboard, clinging to one another in groups, like bees, falling in clusters, in pairs or alone, from a height of about 240 feet, while the main part of the ship tilted upwards at an angle of 65 to 70 degrees. The ship seemed to pause there, suspended, for what seemed like a few minutes. Then, slowly, it turned away from us, as if to hide the tragic spectacle from our eyes.

I looked upward. We were just below the three enormous propellers. For a moment I thought they would crush us. Then, with the terrifying implosion of all its ballast, it gently disappeared into the sea.

When the stern sank, we were sucked toward it, and since we only had one oar, it pulled us closer. It didn't seem to pull very hard however, and most of us decided to remain at the bottom of our raft. At this point we were caught in the middle of much bigger debris floating all around us. The sea was calm and we were able to keep the raft steady, but at any time, a wave could come and sweep us off.

The radio dispatcher was kneeling in water, holding me. We all sang a hymn and said a prayer then waited for dawn. Each time we saw a lifeboat at a distance, we yelled "Ahoy, lifeboat!" But they couldn't distinguish our screams from the others, and we gave up, thinking it was useless. We were very cold and no one could move to get warm as the water splashed over us almost constantly.

Toward dawn, the wind rose and the water became rough, making it harder to keep the raft steady. The radio dispatcher renewed our hopes by telling us that the Carpathia would be here in about three hours. Around 3:30 or 4:00, a few men at the stern of our raft saw the lights of its mast. I couldn't see them because I was sitting, and a man was kneeling on my leg. He finally got up and I got up as well. We had the 2nd Officer, Mr. Lightoller, with us, and he had an officer's whistle. We blew it and the lifeboats in the distance heard and came to rescue us.

It took about an hour and a half for the boats to come. Two of them drew closer. The first took half of us on board and the second one took the rest, of which I was part. During the transfer it was very hard to keep the raft steady, for men were hanging out too far over the sides and we were all taken aboard lifeboats that were already full. Half or three-quarters of an hour later, we were all safely on board the Carpathia."

During this tragedy, the behaviour of some of the passengers was less than honourable. It was said that on the night of the tragedy, a small group of passengers travelling third class got dressed and came to the upper decks seeking safety. A member of the ship's crew tried to restrain them, ordering them to go back to their quarters, but they refused. They were let be, but the doors were then closed with chains and locked to keep others from coming up.

After the Titanic sank, an officer aboard one of the lifeboats proposed that they turn and go back to the scene to save more passengers from drowning. The survivors refused even though their lifeboat was only filled to two-thirds of its capacity. This boat was one of the 36 boats later rescued by the Carpathia, which was sailing that part of the Atlantic that night.

Sir Cosmo Duff Gordon, owner of many stores in London, Paris and New York, embarked, with his wife, in boat #1, which, though it was able to hold up to 40 people, left with only 12 on board. Charles Hendrickson, the captain of the lifeboat, asked his companions in distress if it wouldn't be the right thing to do to help those swimming around them. But Lady Duff Gordon and other passengers voted against it saying it was far too dangerous. And so the 12 survivors on board boat #1 left the scene, condemning hundreds to drown.

Worst of all, the sailors on that same boat complained to Gordon that they had all lost their belongings, and that, very likely, their pay would stop with the sinking of the ship. The rich passengers offered to give the men a sum of money upon their return. This promise was honoured once they were aboard the Carpathia.

In boat #14, a few women pleaded with the officer to distribute his passengers among three other boats and go back to rescue more people. "You should be quite happy to be alive and here on this boat," he replied to them. But he later decided to comply with their request. And Boat #14 was the only lifeboat that went back to rescue others from that scene.

※

In 1892, some 20 years before the Titanic tragedy, the renowned English publicist, William T. Stead, owner of the magazine *Pall Mall Gazette* and founder of *Review of Reviews*, wrote a novel entitled *From the Old to the New World*. This book tells the story of an ocean liner hitting an iceberg and sinking in the North Atlantic. A ship with a captain by the name of E. J. Smith rescues the survivors.

On March 22nd, 1896, Stead published an article entitled *How the Ship Post Sank in the Middle of the Atlantic*. In this story, an unnamed ship crashes into another and, due to a lack of lifeboats, a great number of lives were lost. Stead wrote: "This is exactly what could happen if ships head out to sea without enough lifeboats on board."

Stead was a well-respected man in his time. He was the son of a pastor. Although he had achieved fame and fortune in his career, this did not stop him from using his pen to denounce social injustice. He explored different means of fighting poverty in England, gave his support to the debate on pensions for the elderly, and actively supported the charitable work of the Salvation Army. We are also indebted to him for innovative modern techniques such as adding pictures to newspaper articles.

In 1912, William Stead was asked to give a lecture at an international conference on peace and arbitration at Carnegie Hall in New York. Stead accepted the invitation and decided to travel to America onboard the Titanic. Twenty years after writing his novel, he boarded the Titanic, which was under the command of Edward J. Smith, and he perished with the ship for lack of lifeboats.

In 1898, the American writer Morgan Robertson, through M. G. Mansfield Publishing, released a novel entitled *Futility*, in which an English ocean liner, named *Titan*, hits an iceberg

156

and sinks on its maiden voyage. The tragedy takes place in April in the North Atlantic and the ship does not have enough lifeboats onboard. This imaginary ship, reputed to be unsinkable, is very similar to the Titanic in its dimensions, its speed, and its luxurious furnishings. The number and social status of the passengers onboard the Titan, as well as the number of its victims, is almost identical to that of the Titanic, which sailed 14 years later.

Isaac Frauenthal, a New York lawyer, has a dream before boarding the Titanic at Cherbourg: "I see myself on a huge steamship that suddenly hits something and starts sinking. I hear the screams of fearful passengers." The night of the tragedy, he has the same dream onboard the ship and tells his brother Henry who could not believe it to be possible. He is however on alert when it is announced that the ship has hit an iceberg. Contrary to the way it was with the other passengers, it was easy to convince him to board one of the lifeboats.

During the night of the drama, in the town of Kirbudbright in Scotland, the Salvation Army captain, W. Rex Sowden, is called to the bedside of a dying young orphan name Jessie. At 11:00 p.m., she stood up in her bed despite her condition and said: "Take my hand Captain. I'm so afraid. Do you see the big ship that is sinking?" Sowden tries to comfort her saying it's only a bad dream. "No," she replies, "the ship is sinking. See all those people drowning. Someone named Wally is playing a violin and is coming toward you." Sowden looks around but sees nothing. He lay the little girl in her bed and she went into a coma.

A few hours after Jessie's death, the Titanic sank, while the violinist, Wallace Hartley, and the orchestra he directed kept on playing. Wally Hartley, whom Rex Sowden had known very well when they were children, disappeared in the tragedy. Sowden didn't know he was at sea onboard a ship, on board the Titanic. Wally was on his last travel assignment at sea, after more than 70 transatlantic crossings. He was to be married, but couldn't turn down a very generous offer from the White Star Line. The day before his departure, he wrote his fiancée: "It's a nice ship. We have a good crew and the guys are great. We will be back on a Saturday morning (April 27th) and I'm sure I'll be home by Sunday." Before the launch, he had performed at the Salvage Club in Leeds, his hometown, for the Foundation of Rescue at Sea.

After the collision, while passengers made it to the upper decks, Wallace Hartley continued to lead his orchestra. Many survivors remember that the last piece of music they heard the orchestra play that night was "Nearer, my God, to Thee".

Nearer, my God, to Thee, nearer to Thee!
E'en though it be a cross that raiseth me,
Still all my song shall be, nearer, my God, to Thee.
Nearer, my God, to Thee,
Nearer to Thee!

Though like the wanderer, the sun gone down,
Darkness be over me, my rest a stone.
Yet in my dreams I'd be nearer, my God to Thee.
Nearer, my God, to Thee,
Nearer to Thee!

There let the way appear, steps unto heav'n;
All that Thou sendest me, in mercy giv'n;
Angels to beckon me nearer, my God, to Thee.
Nearer, my God, to Thee,
Nearer to Thee!

Then, with my waking thoughts,
bright with Thy praise,
Out of my stony griefs, Bethel I'll raise;
So by my woes to be nearer, my God, to Thee.
Nearer, my God, to Thee,
Nearer to Thee!

Or, if on joyful wing, cleaving the sky,
Sun, moon, and stars forgot, upward I'll fly,
Still all my song shall be, nearer, my God, to Thee.
Nearer, my God, to Thee,
Nearer to Thee!

There in my Father's home, safe and at rest,
There in my Saviour's love, perfectly blest
Age after age to be, nearer my God to Thee.
Nearer, my God, to Thee,
Nearer to Thee!

It is said that the last passenger to be seen at the tip of the ship, before it sank to the bottom of the icy waters, was William Stead. He was praying, arms toward heaven. Many would say that Stead's prayers were not very useful, neither for him nor for those who were swallowed forever by the ocean!

A few hours prior to the tragedy, Reverend Ernest Carter held a religious service in one of the ship's great saloons. He introduced each hymn with a short history of its composition and the life of its author. Douglas Norman was at the piano and hundreds of voices lifted toward heaven that evening to sing praises to the glory of the eternal God. At around 10 p.m. coffee and cookies were served, then the Reverend Carter concluded with these words: "This is the first time a religious service has been held on this ship, on this Sunday evening, and I pray it is not the last."

All those happy Christians returned to their cabins... and it was the last time that hymns were sung onboard the Titanic.

Among the passengers, there was a Scottish pastor named John Harper who was heading to Chicago to preach in a church. During the sinking of the Titanic, he found himself in the icy ocean waters. While people tried to keep their heads above water, Harper swam from one to the other asking them if they knew Jesus. He asked one of those clinging to a piece of wreckage, about to be carried under by the waves, to entrust himself to Christ. "Believe in the Lord Jesus Christ and you will be saved," Harper quoted. Four years later, at a reunion of the survivors of the Titanic, that same man testified to being saved twice that fateful night. He first received Christ into his life in the icy waters, at the insistence of Harper, and he was later rescued physically from the icy waters.

The ultimate goal of the Reverend Harper was to bring hope to those in despair. It is true that not all that call themselves Christians display such care for the souls of their fellow men. And though the producer of the latest Titanic movie chose to portray those who believe in God as weak and ridiculous, it is only in the hereafter that it will be clearly evident who the weak and ridiculous really were.

The builders of the Titanic claimed that "even God could not sink this ship." They were totally right. God is not the one taking pleasure in sinking ships and watching thousands perish. Captain Smith proudly said: "I cannot imagine a situation where this ship would sink. I cannot conceive of a misfortune hitting this vessel."

It is a grave mistake to think that human beings have an answer to everything and that our intelligence is sufficient to solve the problems of our planet. This haughty assurance can lead a whole society, a whole country to its downfall.

I don't like playing the "prophet of doom," but the legacy of the lessons from history should be taken into consideration more than they are at present. The tragedy of the Titanic is like a modern-day parable. It reminds us that our knowledge, our possessions, our financial security, and our projects can vanish overnight. It also teaches us that our leaders and all that play important roles in our society have to be humble enough to recognize that if human efforts contributing to the well being of people are praiseworthy, humans cannot succeed alone. We need the wise counsel of God.

Jesus said in the Gospel of Mark:

"What good is it for a man to gain the whole world, yet forfeit his soul? Or what will a man give in exchange for his soul? If anyone is ashamed of me and my words in this adulterous and sinful generation, the Son of Man will also be ashamed of him when he comes in his Father's glory with the holy angels."

160

These words may appear harsh, but they are nonetheless true. By rejecting God as we do in our country, we reject the most important thing. We put our faith in human philosophies rather than in his Word, and this has the potential to lead a whole nation to disaster.

My goal is not to criticize society, or our politicians, but to encourage reflection.

Jesus uttered many warnings like these, and this is also part of his love for us. He doesn't want any of us to be lost, and he teaches us that we really need him. He knows we cannot comply perfectly with all of the Bible teachings, but he expects us to turn to him to receive help and walk in his truth. Even though Jesus does not intend to put us down but rather to lift us up, we must take his warnings seriously nevertheless.

What would we say about a father who raised his children without ever teaching them how to behave and without ever warning them of the dangers of their erring ways? We would conclude that he was a bad father.

God is not a bad father. Each human life is precious to him. Those in government, as well as we ourselves, have as our primary responsibility to try and get to know him and abide by his commandments. We should always act in accordance with his directions. We should protect life, whether it be a fetus, or a person who is handicapped, elderly, or suicidal. It should be our goal to preserve life and the principles of God and to see that they are held in high regard everywhere in our country.

I believe that these recommendations apply particularly to artists and the media. We are happy to live in a democracy where there is no way we would think of restraining freedom of expression. However, the freedom of some may affect the freedom of others.

It is not right for artists to communicate destructive messages capable of influencing the morality and thoughts of young people. I believe artists, especially singers, have a strong influence on the morality and thoughts of the youth of Quebec. In that regard, I find that lyrics with a suicidal message such as the one in the song *Partir en Paix (Leaving in*

Peace), can have a very negative impact on young people struggling with depression.

I believe in the potential of many Quebec artists, and I have met some of them and offered them certain books I have published. But this potential should be surrendered to God's love if it is to bear fruit. Not all artists have the courage to openly speak about God in their songs, but those who take that risk have not been discredited for it.

Kevin Parent's song, *"Seigneur"* (*Lord*), won first prize at the ADISQ gala the year of its release, and is a sincere prayer to God. And what about Céline Dion? Hasn't she reached a level of popularity never before attained by a Quebec singer even though she is not ashamed to sing songs with a definite Christian message? Listen to the song *"La mémoire d'Abraham"* (*Abraham's memory*), revealing a very profound truth about God's character.

And her husband, René Angélil, while struggling with cancer, wasn't ashamed to tell journalists: "You know, God is the one who decides." This faith in God did not keep René Angélil from becoming the most successful manager in the province. And though I don't know Céline Dion and René Angélil personally, I rejoice every time a public figure openly affirms his or her faith in God.

I pray that many artists may discover the beauty of God's love, first for themselves, then for others as they communicate this love in their lyrics, unashamed of Jesus or his words. The influence of artists is enormous. They could lead thousands of young people to a personal relationship with God and see their lives transformed by walking with him.

⸎

The story of the Titanic shows us that not only should we avoid the icebergs encountered in the darkness of our nights, but we should also avoid succumbing to our own icebergs. It is a fact that some who survived the Titanic later took their own lives, even after being saved from drowning. They could not appreciate the privilege of having been rescued from the icy waters of death. They never found peace.

Suicide must be observed from a distance and be avoided. To consider suicide a way to find peace is absurd. There is nothing to prove that the sufferings of the soul will end at physical death. If we believe that life goes on after death, we have to consider the possibility that suffering also continues. Isn't that what Jesus tried to teach us when, in the parable of Lazarus and the rich man, he spoke of the torments endured by the latter in the afterlife?

For many this possibility of suffering after death is a myth, a ridiculous concept, a taboo subject we should never entertain, one that religious people have used to manipulate and control the lives of the faithful. And perhaps that is why people don't dare address the topic today!

We should never forget, however, that Jesus spoke about it quite often.

Did he want to be known as a merciless judge, taking pleasure in watching others suffer? I don't think so. I rather think that Jesus wanted to warn us that death doesn't solve anything, that it is not an antidote to inner suffering, and that suicide does not allow the despairing to find rest. Vincent van Gogh understood this fact, but too late. As he lay dying, in the arms of his brother Theo, he breathed these last words: "The sadness will endure."

Imagine if the human soul found itself in a state of immortality, laden with its burdens! What hell! God never wanted it to be so and that's why he came to redeem us, to prove his love to us. This love does not supplant our freedom, however, and we have the choice to either remain in our isolation, or to walk with God.

What happens after death is in reality only the logical consequence of our choices, most particularly the ultimate choice of accepting or rejecting God's friendship. Jesus did everything in order to prove the existence of heaven and to show us that he is the way to get there. We are free to choose whether to believe him or not; he will never force us to believe.

It is God's love for us that drives him to teach us about the realities of the afterlife. The only One who can grant peace and happiness after death is the same One who can transform a desperate situation into a useful experience down here.

In my book of testimonies from ten Quebec doctors, Dr. Serge Chaussé tells how he isolated himself in a cabin in the woods after heartbreak, intending to end his life. It was his darkest hour. But he is alive and happy today because he turned to God and chose life. What his story tells us is that, as difficult as inner sufferings may be here on earth, they do not endure eternally. Dr. Chaussé slowly walked out of his despair and now knows better days. He is remarried and is today a happy man. He found refuge in Jesus.

Dr. Chaussé is currently working on an Internet project in aide of a number of humanitarian endeavours. The difficult period he went through produced in him greater sensitivity to the sufferings of others. He chose to turn to Jesus rather than pull the trigger, and because of his choice, thousands of people have benefited and will benefit from his life.

The walk back from the brink into meaningful life is rarely instantaneous. One has to decide to break the cycle of isolation and talk about their inner turmoil to friends or professional therapists. Recognizing one's need of God and of others is not to be feared. Thousands have found help by calling a help line. This simple action can have a major impact in the life a person in the grip of despair.

The Captain of the Titanic should have paid better attention to the warnings he received by radio. He didn't, and the consequences were tragic. And for us, if we obstinately push God aside and ignore his Word, we also run the risk of shipwreck in our personal and collective lives. It would be profitable to listen to what Jesus has to say. He eagerly desires to walk with us all the way. He never promised that everything would be easy, but he offers his support. Why not make a little more room for him in our day, a special place, and the place a true friend would take…

…A place in our hearts.

Walked straight toward the sea,
Without turning.
Crossed a field, a valley,
The shadow of black spruces
Vanishing in the clearing.
On the trail, step by step,
Footprints disappear.
The prints of men
Greater and more important than I...
God said to me:
"These are men just like you"
And I said:
"These men are just like me"
And I smiled at God.
A crackling noise in the undergrowth.
I shiver.
A domestic cat... a wild cat!
I walk faster.
It must be a domestic cat.
The morning light filters through the trees
And the salt wind mingles
With the fragrance of the pines.
A silvery seagull circles above
To greet me, and relinquish its place...
The ocean awakes.
The world, suddenly deployed at my feet
Engulfs me completely.
I marvel at its beauty, tremble at its strength.
Little pools of water, carved over the centuries,
Between shelves, mirrors of crystal
Like gardens decorated
With multi-colored sea plants,
And golden sand...
I dive in...

C.T.

BAXTER'S HARBOUR

A WARM RAY OF SUN peeks under the hem of the flowered curtain hanging on my bedroom window. Caressing my forehead, it teases my eyelids. I smile as I stretch a little. Today I'll say goodbye to this place.

I slowly place the blanket at the foot of the bed, taking care to properly fold the multi-coloured eiderdown. I open wide all the windows to welcome the warm morning air. The daylight, brilliant, invades the whole interior of my little house. This day is going to be magnificent.

The songs of the chickadees and blue jays, singing hymns to life, never sounded more melodic. Even the bees, their colours in perfect harmony with the goldenrods, add their music to this divine symphony. This beauty from paradise fills me with pure earthy contentment, and I suddenly burst into song.

I had become attached to this rustic little cabin during these past few weeks. Its beauty is charming: the old wood stove with enamel contours chatting with a big tin kettle; the little cupboard displaying in full daylight a multi-ethnic assortment of plates, saucers and cups; two blackened frying pans hanging on the wall side by side like two sisters; a calendar with a picture of the harvest, and another depicting the sea; the blue lamp with its apple-green lampshade, on the corner of the wobbly table where I have put down my pen hundreds of times...

I'm going to miss this place! I did well to come here to write my book, to pour out my grief. I really can't explain it but the words of sadness engraved on my heart little by little became a love song. A song of such beauty that I would like to sing it everywhere.

And I walk to the sea one last time, taking in the beauty of the coast of Nova Scotia.

I came here, to Baxter's Harbour, in King's Valley, to experience peace, to face myself, to meet God... and God was waiting for me. The sea whispered choruses of his love in my ear.

And here I am again, standing before the sea, to say goodbye. What a splendid sight!

The sea is restless. The immaculate foam of its waves gives the impression of a flock of sheep grazing and leaping in a never-ending field of violets. The radiant sky weds its purity to the more passionate blue of the shivering tides. The horizon is perfectly translucent. I can clearly see the shore of the little bay heading to the Minas Basin. Its steep and rocky slopes rise like the walls of a medieval fortress.

The wind caresses my face with tenderness like that of a mother. It gently touches my forehead, teases me, and ruffles my hair. It whispers: "I love you." Its unique fragrance, magical, like a celestial anointing, fills my senses. The pores of my skin open and my soul breathes in the tenderness of this moment.

The sea gulls fly over my head and swirl back as if waving their hands from the tips of their wide wings. They hover low, smiling, then fly away, twirling, emitting brief cries of farewell. They remind me of Micah's drawings, one in particular that he gave me as a birthday gift, and two other drawings the same size. He had carefully mounted them on cardboard frames, giving them the appearance of real paintings. One was of a mill on the shore of a little river; I think he was inspired by the grain mill a few miles from Hébertville. The other one takes us into a beautiful garden filled with multicoloured flowers. The third one was a sketch of a windmill on the seashore. Many white birds glide and twirl, light as little kites, free as the air. They fly very high, making wide invisible circles. These three little pictures were on the wall in our bedroom for years, then they were in my office. I now preserve them preciously in my family picture album.

The sea is singing like a chorus of angels, and listening like a wise old man. I have often gone to the sea to pour out my sorrows and let my soul be rocked. It always understood and comforted me.

During my childhood, the sea was synonymous with treasure islands, adventures and epic voyages on great sailing ships. Coming from an agricultural background as I did, I would dream of the fresh scent of the sea wind, of the taste of salt on my lips, the hot, white sand. I could only imagine the sound of the waves whispering on the beaches as far as the eye could see, the gigantic dunes, and the sea birds hovering above this vast expanse of emerald and turquoise crystal. All these marvels were to be discovered, but I could already feel their beauty.

A few months after my father's death, at age sixteen, I went to Spain. And after crossing the Strait of Gibraltar, I found myself lying on the sand of a Moroccan beach. I stayed there all night, sleeping under the stars. For the first time, I realized that the song of the waves had inhabited my soul ever since the day when, in childlike naiveté, I had placed a huge seashell up to my ear to hear the song of the ocean.

And for the first time, the sea comforted me. It comforted me and gave me little gifts: cone-shaped seashells, and golden sardines, which we grilled on hot coals on the beach, savouring them with salt and lemon. It also gave me the friendship of a few Bedouins who were wandering on the beach with their camels and who invited me into their tent to chat and share a cup of delicious mint tea. Yes, the sea comforted me, playing with me and bringing to life again the joys of my childhood. I was sixteen and the sea became my friend.

A year later I travelled to the coast of California, north of San Francisco. I had travelled through the night, and in the

169

morning the sea was the first to welcome me. It was bordered with green hills where sheep were grazing, and this time it offered me the gift of a huge abalone shellfish, adorned with pearly jewels. It was as if I held a rainbow in the palm of my hand.

Another time I found myself alone with the sea in the south of Mexico, near Guatemala. It welcomed me warmly. One after another her waves threw themselves upon me as if to embrace me. We laughed and played for a long time. Then one evening as I swayed in my hammock, listening to her melodies, it seemed to me that her song contained a few sad notes. Listening intently, I sensed she wanted to reveal her secrets to me.

That evening, the sea spoke to me for a long time. She spoke of the misery of the poor peasants, working from dawn to dusk for meager wages. She spoke of the distress of the women of Oaxaca, walking barefoot in the mountains, carrying their babies on their backs, forced to seek food for two little orphans abandoned by their fathers. She showed me children in rags, sick, receiving no care; drunken fishermen constantly swearing; young teenage girls, pregnant and left to fend for themselves. The sea told me about the sufferings of mankind… and that evening, the sea and I cried.

And many years passed before I could go back to the sea. When I saw the beaches of the Gaspé in the distance, I was happy to be there, along with my four children. The sea also rejoiced, and gave us hundred of gifts: pebbles of all shapes and colours, agates which we held up to the sun to see their transparent beauty, sand castles with high overlapping towers, and a multitude of vigorous fish biting our hooks during spawning season.

I can see my children again, on the shore, near Percé Rock on a gorgeous sunny afternoon. It was the first time we went together to explore this enormous rock, pictured on so many postcards of the Gaspé region. The tide was low, and we headed out cheerfully toward the gigantic mass of rock, pierced through over time by the waves. Micah and Annie went on ahead while I came behind with the two smaller children. We reached the rock but the mounting tide took us by surprise and, along with the remaining tourists, we had to retreat in a hurry. We all got drenched to the waist. What an experience!

Further down the beach, I asked a passerby to take a picture of us with my camera. I placed this beautiful souvenir on a poster board in my office. It was the last time I went to the sea with my children.

⟫⟪

Now I find myself on the coast of the Bay of Fundy, where the tides are the highest in the world. It is said they can reach as high as 55 feet. Once more the sea is my confidante and friend. She offered me her treasures: more pebbles for my collection, a royal landscape, the solitude I needed, and... the pages of a book that I hope will bring comfort to my children's hearts and to the hearts of many others.

It seems that the more I know the sea, the more it speaks to me about God. I think they surely have some kind of connection.

I have always been fascinated with the passage of Scripture where, after his crucifixion and resurrection, Jesus is on the beach, alone, frying fish for his friends who are still at sea pulling their nets out of the water. Jesus waits for them by the shore. preparing to share a meal with them. He wants to see the faces of these rugged fishermen, sitting around the fire once more. He particularly wants to see Peter again, Peter who had denied him so vociferously a few days before. He knows that Simon Peter's tender heart is crumbling under a heavy load of guilt, and that is why Jesus wants so much to talk to him. He wants to eat with him, and look him straight in the eye, put his hand on his shoulder and say: "Peter, I know you love me and regret what you did. Now, if you want to, let's start over. I will never abandon you."

Even if we want to believe that "men don't cry," I'm convinced that Jesus and Peter cried that day. And hugged. What joy for Jesus to see that the price he paid to reconcile mankind

171

was not in vain. It is a price that neither Peter, nor you, nor I could ever pay. All we can do is offer our lives to him in an act of gratitude.

For too long this biblical truth has been like a grain of sand in my oyster shell. It cut into my flesh. But when my brokenness began to surround this intruder, it became clear that God was in the process of forming a pearl. I understood that daily struggles could be redeemed and transformed into something beautiful by the hand of God. I could see that this world's tragedies were not God's doing. As I watched the sea, I realized that the high tides of anguish and depression are not eternal. They can reach frightening heights, but sooner or later, they recede!

I leave the beach a bit against my will. I experienced such intense moments with God here that it has become a sacred place. I'm only saying "so long", for I wish to return next year with my daughters to share with them the overwhelming beauty of this place.

Thinking about my beloved daughters, I am reminded of a conversation I had with Annie the other day when she remembered an illustration I had used years ago for a lecture:

A teenager, walking along the beach, watches hundreds of starfish that the waves keep sweeping onto the shore. Some make it back to the salty water, but many barely limp along without hope of ever reaching the sea again. The young man's heart is stirred as he watches the tragedy playing out before him. He peers into the distance, the beach stretching endlessly before him. He doesn't know how many starfish he will be able to rescue, but one by one he starts carrying those beautiful creatures back to the ocean.

Farther up the beach, he meets a few classmates who mock him for wasting his time rescuing simple starfish. "What difference is it going to make?" they ask.

Calmly the young man picks up a starfish and says to them: "I may not be able to help all of them since there are so many thrown up on the beach and left to die. But I can assure you that for this one here in my hand, my action will make all the difference in the world."

Then walking to the water's edge, he gently releases the starfish.

Like that courageous young man, I too want my actions to make a difference, in the lives of my children, in the lives of the people around me, and in the lives of the greater human family. One way is through a book. For others it will be through a smile, a prayer, a friendly letter, a bouquet of flowers, an evening at the movies, or any other of the many little things that make life better for others. There is truth in the saying that "…it is more blessed to give…" Each one of us can contribute something to society to make it better. We can make a difference, even if it is for only one person. Or even for ourselves.

❧

Across the road is a small church, apparently abandoned. I had noticed it every time I used this road to get to the sea, but had never stopped to visit it. It looks like most little countryside chapels except that this one is particularly old. There is a padlock on the door, which tells me the parishioners have forgotten about it. Treading softly, I walk around it till I get to a window. I take a peek inside, shielding my eyes from the sun with both hands beside my face.

I imagine those good peasants, farmers and fishermen, sitting with their families on the wooden benches, hands joined in prayer while the pastor's wife plays the old piano. And there is the dusty pulpit on which the pastor must have laid his Bible so many times before he preached, simply but with conviction.

On one of the walls of the church hangs a large painting of Jesus, the Good Shepherd. I always liked the works decorating the interiors of old churches. The frescoes in the church of the little village where I grew up had more impact on my childhood spirituality than all the priest's sermons. They were probably good sermons, but I can't recall a single word he spoke from the pulpit. And I vividly remember the paintings illustrating Jesus' life.

The picture of the Good Shepherd in this little church reveals a very particular aspect of Jesus' life. I never saw anything like it before. This painter must have been close to the people here, because he not only represented Jesus as the shepherd of the flock, but he also gave him the appearance of a great lighthouse, like those found off the coast of the Bay of Fundy. Jesus is thus the shepherd who tends his flock, but also the light that shines in the darkness.

Turning around, I notice that behind the church is a little cemetery bordering a forest. I slowly make my way to it. I open the small iron gate at the entrance and shut it behind me. I stay motionless for a moment, and my thoughts turn once again to Micah. I walk solemnly among the tombstones, reading the few words inscribed to the memory of the beloved ones.

Here, the name of James L. Benjamin, with these simple words: Born in the USA. Close by, on another tombstone, the name of George McCulley and his spouse, Alice Jane McCulley. A little farther, Allen Victor Schofield, 1954-1974, asleep in Jesus. He was only 20, one year older than Micah. Then this other epitaph on the tomb of an eighteen-year-old girl, Carol Ruth Barkhouse, 1941-1959, Forever in our memories — Forever in our hearts.

I brush away a tear. I feel the intense sorrow of the parents who saw their beloved daughter leave so soon in life. I think of Micah who also left at a young age, and I feel close to these parents. I feel close to all parents who have lost a child. I find relief in having received from the Lord the conviction that death is not the ultimate end, that life continues in the afterlife, and that a multitude of people are rejoicing in heaven in the presence of Jesus for all eternity. It is the blessed hope of the Christian faith, which brings the deepest consolation to those left behind. Life on this earth is but a journey, and it is a short one. However long mine lasts, I want it always to be a close walk with God. May it be lived intensely and reach a happy fullness of years.

The Lord is my shepherd and I know that even through the darkest of nights, he will be there with me, to comfort and protect me, and to shine his light on my path. I want to live my life one day at a time, with my eyes fixed on this light that shines like a star in the night, the Morning Star.

I know that one day, guided by my Savior's love, I will dock safely at the heavenly harbour, welcomed by a crowd of happy people. I know I will see Jesus in all his splendour. I also know that I will see the young man my heart so deeply loves, my beautiful Micah. I think he will run to me just as I will run to him. And as two friends separated for too long, we will embrace for a long time, crying in each other's arms.

This time, they will be tears of joy!

A sculpture is inert.
My goal is to bring it to life
and validate that life.
I form my great compositions
As dynamically as I can
and I colour them
Because I want them to appeal
and plead
To other human beings.

RAYMOND MASON

THE ILLUMINATED CROWD

THIS CHAPTER WAS ORIGINALLY intended to be the conclusion to my book, a short and modest conclusion. Leaving Baxter's Harbour, I had a good idea of what those last paragraphs would say. But once back home, a pile of work awaited me on my desk, forcing me to leave the manuscript in its folder. Days go by, the work keeps increasing and the writer's inspiration slumbers in the shade of urgent matters. Days become weeks …then months.

Here we are at the end of January. Christmas balls and garlands are once again in their boxes at the back of the closet. I spent beautiful days with my daughters: we celebrated Christmas together as a family and took a few hikes in the forest on our snowshoes. It was so wonderful!

There is a lot of snow this year. The fir trees are laden with snow like a thick layer of cotton and the picnic table in the back yard can barely be seen under the snow; in some places, it is twelve feet deep. Our house is by a lake and from my window I marvel at the huge basin of water, turned into thick ice. From time to time a fisherman comes, drills a hole in the ice and sets up his fishing lines in the hopes of catching a trout or a bass. Often the wind blows the powdery snow away playfully and the lake then becomes a vast skating rink. I like to wrap myself in a long coat, put a scarf around my neck, and brave the storm just to listen to the whistling of the wind, as heaven and earth melt into one.

But the most beautiful Canadian winter scenes occur on warmer days when the trees of the forest are covered with frost. This surreal beauty is hard to imagine for those who have never witnessed this unique feature of the northern climate. Each immaculate twig, each branch, shivers, so frail that you feel it could break with the slightest movement. The cold then brings a light fog and the first rays of the sun add to this fresco the breathtaking yellow and blue hues. The snow glitters like a mantle of white satin sprinkled with diamonds among the silvery birches. The trees are all white. A white forest, bathed in light. A magical country where angels could appear at any moment. Each tree becomes a burning bush, beaming with a blinding purity. Even though stripped of their colorful summer apparel, they are still majestically clothed.

White drizzle clouds the view somewhat. The snow muffles all sound. An indescribable peace emanates from this kingdom. I walk alone, completely wrapped in God's presence.

Silence beckons me, like a writer's white page, like a virgin canvas before the painter, inviting me to create, to give, to paint colours on the canvas, unique colours, colours I would chose. He invites me to let my words flow onto this white page, simple words, tender ones, words of sadness and pain but also words of love that I can offer at will, like a bouquet of flowers.

God's presence doesn't impose, but rather comes to me freely. I am not expected to do anything, the Presence is just here. Even with the cold all around me, its fire burns in my soul. Even in my solitude, this presence floods me; even in silence, it speaks to me. And Creation eloquently speaks of God's greatness, providing me with the words to express my gratitude.

I look at the tall oaks whose branches spread out like the wings of a dove. They lift their feathers towards heaven in the midst of the storm. They teach me that in spite their nakedness, in spite of the cold, it is possible to keep a grateful heart.

When night falls on the frosty woods and the moon slowly removes its veil, the enchanted forest once again offers a marvelous sight. Thick icy frost covers the trees, turning the forest into a silvery-blue crystal fairyland. Timidly the night creatures, the fawns, the deer, the snowy owl, all come out of hiding and move about under the stars.

⇒≫≪⇐

Winter is losing its grip now. The cold of February defers to the more friendly weather of March. The sun is more at ease and postpones it's departure more and more each day. I think often about my manuscript and don't understand what paralyzes me. It sits on a shelf near my desk, but I can only glance at it. Inspiration has fled, and I can only wait for it to return.

My fingers run rapidly over the computer keyboard. It is Thursday morning and the sky is rather dark. A friend phones with news that hits me like a thunderbolt: "I think I found the source of inspiration for Micah's drawings," he says. "I don't have all the details, but the sculpture is somewhere on McGill Avenue in Montreal, near the Bank of Paris building."

My thoughts run wild, and a strong feeling of anticipation mixed with nostalgia and joy rushes through me.

Micah used to browse through picture books and reproduce the scenes that moved him. But until now, I didn't know if the source of his inspiration had been a painting, a sculpture, or simply something he sketched while standing before a work of art.

Without hesitation, I call the Bank of Paris in Montreal to speak with the receptionist and get more precise information. As I speak with her, my heart swells with emotion.

I describe to her the three characters drawn by Micah and she immediately recognizes them. She confirms they are part of an imposing sculpture that stands four levels high on the esplanade of the Louis Dreyfus Group building, located at 1981 McGill College Avenue.

I can hardly believe it. I must go there at once and see this work of art. A thousand questions suddenly surface. Did Micah find this sculpture in downtown Montreal, or in a library book? Why did he only draw three of the characters?

And what directed his choice toward these and not the others? What was their significance for Micah? Would my interpretation be true to Micah's? And what about the sculptor, would he approve?

It is impossible now for me to concentrate on my work. So I drop everything and get in touch with the information desk of the building on McGill College to find out more about the sculpture. What a joy to contact this kind woman who offers immediately to fax me the pages of a small brochure entitled *The Illuminated Crowd*. The illuminated crowd! I stand waiting, impatient for the first fax to arrive. First it's only text, then another page of text, and then... a picture! Dark, but as I grab it, my eyes recognize it at a glance.

Though I can't make out all the details of each character, I can clearly distinguish the forms of the three that Micah drew. My heart races. I must make my way to Montreal, at all cost!

I rush to the local library to gather more information about the artist and this work. Raymond Mason, the sculptor, is from Birmingham, England. He is known for his outdoor sculptures relating to urban life. He is also known as a sensitive man, close to the poor and the humble, feeling their joys and sorrows. His work speaks of theirs.

In a book dedicated to this great sculptor, Michael Edwards writes "the first contact with the work of Raymond Mason — or with the man himself — can provoke an intense and lasting surprise."

The Illuminated Crowd is the most ambitious of all his works. It is a grouping of 65 characters, with light shining on them from a horizontal angle. The light fades into the crowd, and the weaker it gets, the heavier is the sense of loss. The figures are set on four ascending panels. Mason is said to have planned to write on these panels the words: illumination, hope, interest, hilarity, irritation, fear, sickness, violence, murder, and death.

The three figures in Micah's drawing are from the last panel, the lowest one, and the one corresponding to death!

The great skyscrapers of Montreal emerge on the horizon. I awake early this morning and the shadows of the night dissipate as I leave the highway to enter the folds of the awakening city. As in the past, it greets me warmly. The sky is blue and clear. The sun touches the skyscrapers, reflecting the pink, blue, turquoise, and silver shades of their mirror-like façades. They look like cathedrals. And the big stone churches nearby don't seem to mind.

I drive up University Street and cross René-Lévesque Boulevard. The addresses scroll by: 900, 1200 ...I'm getting closer. A great painted mural on the brick wall of a building attracts my attention. It blends well with the colors of the luxury hotel next to it.

The scene now resembles an old downtown market. Women with long orange and yellow dresses; another woman in a blue dress and white blouse, and a little round hat on her head; all around are big wooden barrels filled with apples, peaches and assorted vegetables; two men with top hats walk behind, preceded by two children; on the left, a photographer with one of those old cameras is about to immortalize the beauty of it all.

The numbers are getting higher. I'm almost there!

From the chimney of a factory, a line of white smoke reaches for the sky, steady as those coming from the small country houses depicted by certain painters.

Montrealers are on their way to work. Some walk swiftly, others are talking together. Here and there workers wait for the bus, sipping their hot coffee. A businessman in a suit almost runs along the sidewalk, with his cellular phone in hand. White men and women, Asians and Arabs, move along in all directions. They seem happy! A taxi driver from Haiti cruises along St. Catherine Street. An old Polish woman crosses without looking. An old man claps his mittens to warm his hands. Teenagers tease and jostle each other in a schoolyard.

I am close! I park my car on President Kennedy Avenue, and I walk to McGill College Avenue. I don't know how to describe my emotions. I think of Micah and feel a deep nostalgia that brings me to tears. At the same time, I am like a little boy making his way to the country fair, impatient to experience the most intense moments of his young life. I cut across the shadow of a few tall buildings, and I glimpse the street sign for McGill College and …there, suddenly, *The Illuminated Crowd!*

It is magnificent beyond my expectations. Standing at the foot of a beautiful building that reaches high in the sky, it is both small and huge at the same time. Its towers form a fortress-like wall, suggesting a clearing in the middle of a forest where some people have stopped. The sculpture's light ochre colour sings against the bluish windows of the building.

Was it a coincidence or of divine prompting? At the precise moment that I reach the sculpture, a ray of sun finds its way between the neighbouring buildings, splashes against the windows of the Louis Dreyfus Group Building, and reflects its light with the intensity of a spotlight on the three figures of the lowest panel — the ones Micah drew.

I am close to the figures, and I feel the same light penetrate my soul. It was as if a great curtain lifted on an epic scene and the sudden revealing of a grand stage on which stood a tableau of actors. Breathlessly I reach out and touch the three figures. I cannot hold back the tears. I gaze at them! Thousands of lights illuminate my spirit, in an instant shedding light on all my questions

I slowly walk around the four panels on which *The Illuminated Crowd* is placed and I admire the strength of expression Mason gave each of his figures. An entire day wouldn't be sufficient time for me to appreciate the power of the message they communicate.

As the name says, this is a work where light plays a primary role. The concept came to Mason while watching a crowd during fireworks in Paris. The figures in the forefront are bathed in daylight. They look ahead. The central figure is a man with his arm outstretched, finger pointing to a distant source of the light. His eyes, like those of the man he's talking to, are sunken in their orbit. Yet they are different from the eyes of the other characters, as if they could actually see something the others are only looking at.

Mason says that the extended arm of the central figure encroaches on the sidewalk in order to "command the attention of the passersby." It calls out to them to change their state of mind from one of just "looking" to one of "seeing." To quote Michael Edwards: "The man with the outstretched arm is also the man who, like people everywhere, asks a question, by his prolonged gaze, and by the scope, so to speak, of his gesture… His outstretched arm is a sign of life, but what it points to remains unknown."

Near those two men, a woman holds her son, an old man puts his arm around his wife's waist, and a father carries his daughter on his shoulders. The mouths of some are opened, as if thirsty for light. A woman nestles her head against her husband's shoulder in an expression of pure happiness. Crouched in front of them, a little bald man, fearful, doesn't dare get up. He hides behind the man with the outstretched arm, risking only a timid glance toward the light.

Signs of what Mason calls, "our decaying nature," are already evident in the foreground of the sculpture. Like the decaying of nature, the light also fades as it progresses through the crowd. The characters on the second panel are in the shadows and the faces start to look away. Amazement gives way to mockery and indifference. A Buddhist monk closes his eyes beside an angry man who screams insults at a little child looking for his parents in the crowd.

Seeing this, I climb onto the second level between the figures to reach the child. I want to stand at his level, and see with his eyes. I want to be one with this crowd… me, the orphan, rejected and misunderstood.

The little child tries to make his way through this world of "big people", hostile and indifferent. He turns his back on the third level and closes his right eye so as not to see the evil, the violence, the sickness, the rape and the murder that is played out there.

Turning to reach the third level, I come face-to-face with a man who is running into the crowd, his hand pointing toward heaven. It looks as if he is attempting to draw attention to something. Maybe he carries good news, or perhaps bad. Maybe he carries an admonition or a warning. But he runs into an angry man who appears to be about to silence him.

Those two men remind me of the biblical story of the blind man, Bartimeus, who yells with all his might to attract Jesus' attention, while the offended crowd orders him to keep quiet. Fortunately he pays no attention to the crowd, and because of his perseverance he receives what he seeks from the Master.

But this hand above the crowd may also be one of distress, a hand that penetrates the waves of human decay, seeking for help.

On the opposite side of the third level, four sick men collapse one after the other, as one.

The majority of the figures on this level are looking either to the right or to the back. None can see the light. Towering over all the characters of this panel is a man, with a blank stare. He stands half in the light and half in the shadow, looking neither ahead nor behind. His neutrality raises the thought: Can one stay neutral and passive when all around him is crumbling?

And this evil persists as we make our way through the sculpture. A strange character, masked and armed with a knife, is about to sacrifice his victim, a half-naked woman he's holding by the wrist. Behind him rises a thick patch of smoke from a smokestack, leading to the fourth level.

Mason says that the crowd loses its way: "Feeling is lost. The violence seen in the hearts of the crowd speaks of the frailty and weakness of our species. And all ends in darkness, the ultimate result of decay." Mason adds that this deterioration of his subject is "its descent into hell."

This cloud of smoke is found in other works by Mason. In one of them, (I think it is part of *Forward,* a work exhibited in Birmingham, England), the cloud literally swallows a

184

man crying for help, his hand reaching heavenward. In that sculpture, it is the smoke coming from a factory that poisons and pollutes the life of the citizens. But in *The Illuminated Crowd*, it is a smoke we could call "hellish," a smoke directly linked to death. It is the smoke described in the book of Revelation, coming up from the abyss to eradicate the human race.

Finally, on the fourth level, there are only four characters: The three characters of Micah's drawing, with another man lying down on the platform, agonizing, or already dead.

⇒»«⇐

Mason's work didn't always receive favorable reviews from the critics. Many seemed to be unaware of their meaning or unable to catch the message the artist tried to convey. For example, Michael Brenson, critic for the New York Times, wrote concerning *The Illuminated Crowd*:

"Mason's human comedy is now complete; for the first time, he brings together the destitute and the blessed, the damned and the chosen. It is human comedy in its purest expression, undiluted, isolated from anything that could position and explain it."

Fortunately, Edwards, in his book devoted to Mason, dares to bring a few "explanations" to this sculpture. He identifies important themes like light and darkness, life, death and hell. He is, however, unable to be clear when it comes to answering the most crucial questions this work provokes. "The idea might be Promethean, but Mason seems to catch, in the project and beyond it, in the idea and beyond it, a glimpse of the presence of something else, a superior force that we had better not name."

It is unfortunate to note the extent to which our society goes to avoid frank and honest dialogue about God. Even in the debate surrounding suicide and its prevention, I find it regrettable that there is an effort made to avoid addressing anything pertaining to God. The very subject is taboo. We do nevertheless face questions concerning life, death and the afterlife.

The discomfort surrounding the teachings and the person of Christ should be addressed as soon as possible. The phobia towards Christianity only worsens our state.

Edwards asks the right question but he doesn't answer it.

"It is important that the light remain undefined. For if there is one question this work asks more precisely than the others, it is the same supreme question Mason often mentions in his interviews: Given the obvious disappearance of the Christian religion from the 18th century on, what other faith is great enough to embrace and articulate the whole of mankind's destiny? And with the loss of Christian history, what other topic is sufficiently true and universal to command the highest and most dedicated efforts of the arts?"

There is none! No faith, no subject, as deep as it may be, can ever replace the Christian faith!

Isn't refusing to name the source of the light the same as ignoring it? Isn't turning away from the Biblical accounts equal to denying Christ? And if he was the only true light, doesn't our refusal to admit it plunge us into darkness and death?

In an interview, Mason said once that "painting [he could have said sculpting] is an act of worship." Those words open a window on the faith that inhabits the soul of this great artist. It appears evident to me that this work of art before me, this crowd illuminated by the light that shines between the skyscrapers of downtown Montreal, offers answers to many of our most fundamental questions.

And the ultimate answer is found on the fourth platform, among the characters that Edwards identified as the "hub of the work", the figures Micah had sketched.

⇒》《⇐

"Your power is broken;
No one will come to cut us down now!...
In the place of the dead

there is excitement over your arrival.
World leaders and mighty kings long dead
are there to see you.
With one voice they all cry out,
`Now you are as weak as we are!
Your might and power are gone;
they were buried with you.
All the pleasant music in your palace has ceased.
Now maggots are your sheet
and worms your blanket.
How you are fallen from heaven,
O shining star, son of the morning!
You have been thrown down to the earth,
you who destroyed the nations of the world.
For you said to yourself, I will ascend to heaven
and set my throne above God's stars.
I will preside on the mountain of the gods
far away in the north.
I will climb to the highest heavens
and be like the Most High.
But instead, you will be brought down
to the place of the dead, down to its lowest depths.
Everyone there will stare at you and ask,
Can this be the one who shook the earth
and the kingdoms of the world?
Is this the one who destroyed the world
and made it into a wilderness?"

EXCERPTS FROM ISAIAH CH.14

The man with a heart of stone is sitting at the threshold of hell, waiting for his victims. His eyes reveal his evil spirit. He has injected his venom into the entire human race, and all he has to do is wait for the poison to do its work.

Mason planned to write on this fourth level the word "obscurantism." This man with a heart of stone wears a turban. He represents the prince of darkness the Gospels speak about. Unable to accomplish any saving act, he penetrates our

187

conscience to add darkness and destruction to our misery. He lives in a parallel world but his influence can be felt all around us. It is he who urges us to remain cold before situations that require our intervention, our help, our efforts, our encouragement, our smile and our warmth. He teaches us to be like him: a man with a heart of stone.

He teaches us to be indifferent to those who are close to us, to despise our neighbours, our co-workers, our rivals and our classmates. He shows us how to destroy the self-esteem of others; how to turn our backs on those who offer their love, however clumsily, be it a member of our family or a friend. He locks us in our prisons. And in our isolation, our wounds become infected, forgiveness fades, and death moves in. He kills the child in us, our spontaneity, our transparency, our beauty. He chokes our sense of wonder and our purity. He darkens our dreams and throws his rubbish on us, defiling the intimacy of our daily lives. He sows the seeds of revolt, against others, against ourselves, against God. He robs our minds of the true light and plunges our spirit into a world of illusion and darkness.

C. S. Lewis, in his book, *The Lion, The Witch, and the Wardrobe* rightly describes the angel of darkness as a witch who turns all of her rebellious subjects into stone statues. The man with a heart of stone will never be able to change the world, for he himself is prisoner of darkness and evil.

Since October, when a lightning bolt announced,
on relatively short notice, the imminent end
of my earthly pilgrimage,
my thoughts, have turned toward things
loving and eternal.
Now I have the joy of contemplating that time
when I will be in direct contact with the Father,
the Son and the Holy Spirit,
knowing that on the other side of faith
I will have the answer to my questions,
and I will bathe in the unending joy
of light, of truth and of love.
I continually give thanks to Jesus
for his teaching
that guided, protected, and directed me
to the love of God
and love for my fellow humans,
particularly the sick, the destitute,
and those who hunger and thirst
For righteousness.
How can I not thank him for the Redemption
that led him to endure for us
the whipping, the crown of thorns,
carrying his Cross, the crucifixion,
and giving his life
to wash us from all our sins,
then rising from the dead to open the doors
of the eternal Kingdom
where all is joy and fullness of Love?

CAMILLE LAURIN
(Secretary of State in Quebec's Government, from 1976-1984)
(Excerpt from a letter to his wife)

THE SAVIOUR

THE FINAL VERSION of *The Illuminated Crowd*, now installed in downtown Montreal, is the second sculpture of a large crowd by Raymond Mason. The first one, created in 1963, was the culmination of all the street scenes that had absorbed this important city dweller. In it, nearly one hundred figures appear to descend on the onlooker.

This bronze work was displayed at the Pierre Matisse Art Gallery in New York. It was later purchased by France and now stands in the garden of Les Tuileries, in Paris, barely 500 feet from the Place de la Concorde. Another group sculpture, created by Mason in 1969, is entitled Le Départ des Fruits et Légumes du Cœur de Paris (*When Fruit and Vegetables Left the Heart of Paris*). The theme exposes the sadness of the market-gardeners at being banned from the center of Paris.

A few years later, in 1974, Mason learned of a mining tragedy that had occurred in Liévin, near Lens, in France. The article had a photo showing miners' family members waiting in anguish at the entrance of the mine for news of the their loved ones. Mason, inspired by that picture, created a dreadful northern winter scene bathed in tears and rain. He called the work, *A Northern Tragedy*.

He also created an urban sculpture for the city of Washington. The sculpture is in two sections. On its lower level is a group of people from our time looking at a wall in front of them, a pensive representation of the American War of Independence. The scene is of Major Pierre Charles l'Enfant showing his friend, George Washington, the plans of the city that he intends to build and which will bear Washington's name.

"I think people have lost track of what life is truly about," said Mason in reply to a clumsily worded question implying that his work resembled *L'Opéra des Gueux*. I, too, think that people have forgotten about the sacredness of life. We live in a world where industrialization, materialism, and individualism have crushed the beauty of true social values, and are about to overwhelm the ecological system of our planet.

It is this reality Mason portrays in his works. To me, the light radiating from *The Illuminated Crowd* is different from the fireworks scene he first drew inspiration from. This is not about the fleeting glow of fireworks, no matter how colourfully projected on the stage of an outdoor sky, nor the best human ideals fading at twilight. All of this seems too shallow to represent the powerful message this sensitive sculptor tried to transmit to us.

No, the light shining on Mason's crowd reveals the degeneration of the human race. And even if the figures in the foreground express serenity at first, on examining the work carefully we realize that their eyes are not really seeing the light, they are blinded by the darkness in their souls.

The truth is that the true light is seen not from standing in front of the sculpture, but from behind it. Standing at the edge of the fourth level, our perception changes, and Mason's work takes on a new meaning.

Welcomed by the honest gaze of a man whose peaceful features stand out from this violent, wandering crowd, I regain my courage and become the student of this character who immediately gained my trust. This bearded man, leaning on the edge of the third level, peers into the horizon with confidence. He reminds me of the captain of a ship, proud and experienced. Or one of those sculpted figures on the prow of ancient ships, braving the worst storms.

What is strange is that this man gives the impression that he is carrying the whole crowd on his shoulders, without collapsing!

192

This character could, of course, portray the sculptor unveiling his work to us. He could also be, as I see him, the image of a father, trying to make sense of death... starting with his son's death.

However, the amplitude of the human tragedy unveiled by Mason demands an answer that transcends our daily business and concerns, an answer that can satisfy the human soul, thirsty for light and truth.

This character is God himself, the Creator of the universe, who carries on his shoulders the burden of the entire human race. He looks at the scene of death as it is portrayed on the last level, and he is completely calm. The emotion emanating from him is not one of despair; his eyes, far from being glued to the corpse before him, seem to be aware of something beyond this gloomy scene. His inner strength is not indifferent. On the contrary, his face suggests greatness, like that of the most glorious yet humble warrior. His eyes tell us that he is the answer to all questions, and that he has conquered all enemies, even death.

I walk around the sculpture once more, and this time I stand on the left side of the fourth level. From this angle, I notice that the face of the bearded man and the man I nicknamed "the traveller" are almost at the same level. An incredible bond of complicity has developed between the two.

The traveller is a black man who exudes compassion. His gaze is not a sideways glance at the Hindu sitting on his left, as I first thought from Micah's drawing, but he is looking straight ahead with a look of determination. The old man and the traveller are not looking at each other but they share the same indescribable expression — one that fills me with deep respect. It is an expression akin to perfect complicity, of strength and assurance from another world, found on no other figure portrayed in this crowd. Their unity of spirit is so real that one wonders if they are not the same man, in different roles.

It's as if the old captain became the narrator of the scene that is unfolding on the fourth level, inviting all passersby, all spectators, and the entire human race, to set their eyes on the central figure of the work.

And the traveller moves along with assurance, his eyes looking straight ahead. He is about to cross all the levels of human history, rekindling hope for all of Creation. He will make his way through the crowd, not to make a place for himself among the great, where vanity and the law of the strong reign, but rather to declare that he himself is the light of the world and its Saviour. The traveller's only preoccupation is to carry his wounded one toward the healing light of God's love. And he will succeed!

The wounded one is therefore in good hands. He is no longer carrying the weight of his misery alone, but he lets himself be carried by the One who has freed him from the clutches of death.

Even with his eyes half-open, the wounded one is the only figure looking in the same direction as the old man. It is as if he has agreed to exchange the desperate vision of his own degeneration for the vision of God the Father, who is looking down upon the redemptive act of his Son. There is truly no other way to salvation.

Any spirituality that ignores the revelation of salvation through the work of God's Son is futile. Placing Christianity among the world's "great religions" and honouring Christ as "one of the great masters", is far from Jesus' teaching. He said, "I am the way, the truth, and the life. No one comes to the Father but by me."

And, if the man with a turban represented the whole of the world's religions and human philosophies, we could respectfully declare that he still has no power to save anyone. It is impossible for humans to climb a stairway to heaven, despite our efforts and good will. It is impossible because those stairs have already been climbed, but in the opposite direction. God himself came down to us, and to ascend the stairs to the heavenly temple, we must allow ourselves to be carried by him.

No other can carry us this way. And the so-called "spiritual guides" that some religions suggest are of no real help.

Neither angels, nor our departed loved ones are authorized to play this role of guide and saviour. The Bible severely warns us not to try to get in touch with the dead. Jesus Christ is the One we have to address, and no other. He is the only Saviour.

Looking at Micah's drawing now no longer crushes me. This guilt that attempted to draw me to death is no longer weighing on my conscience. This drawing has become proof of divine love to me. It no longer represents agony and death, but salvation given by God to the suffering soul. A salvation that Micah fortunately received during the last minutes of his life.

Looking at the traveller, I no longer address him as such; I now call him Saviour. A Saviour who proved his love by lowering himself, in order to fully engage in relationship with me. He gave his life to save me from death. A Saviour, completely stripped of everything, like the wounded one he's carrying. He identifies with me completely, becoming human to prove his love for me. He experienced the depths of hell and conquered hell. He gave his life, as a ransom to pay my debt toward God, a debt that man could never pay. God himself took care of it… but at what a price!

A magnificent poem that is taken from the epistle to the Philippians illustrates this mystery. It is said to be a hymn that was sung by first century Christians. A hymn that neither history nor people can destroy. A hymn that believers throughout history, in the company of countless numbers of angels, will one day sing together before the throne of God:

Jesus Christ, being in very nature God,
did not consider equality with God
something to be grasped,
but made himself nothing,
taking the very nature of a servant,
being made in human likeness.

And being found in appearance as a man,
He humbled himself
and became obedient to death
even death on a cross!
Therefore God exalted him to the highest place

and gave him the name that is above every name,
that at the name of Jesus every knee should bow,
in heaven and on earth and under the earth,
and every tongue confess that Jesus Christ is Lord,
to the glory of God the Father.

EPISTLE TO THE PHILIPPIANS, CHAPTER 2

I firmly believe that we will one day meet again with all those who love God and have received his forgiveness. It will be the most beautiful reunion. During our earthly pilgrimage, however, it is his love that will sustain us every moment of our lives.

As for me, I have an appointment with a young man living within the walls of that heavenly city. He is waiting for me there, and I believe that upon my arrival, we will embrace each other silently, and for a long time …simply savouring the joy of being together again. God loaned him to me for a time here on earth so that I would experience the joy and the pride of being his father. However, though death won one "round", it didn't win the whole "fight". The sadness, the grief and the anger that were in me have been changed into a fire of divine love, thrusting me back into the spiritual battle with divine strength.

In the face of death, as King Solomon said, the wise man reflects. The loss of my son constantly places me before the reality of death. I do not want to play the role of "saviour" because Jesus is the only Saviour. But this Jesus lives in me! I often think of the number of people who die every day without having been reconciled to God, and I think about the story of the starfish agonizing on the sand.

And I tell myself that if I can take even one of those little creatures among the thousands dying there on the beach and carry it to the water… for that one, it will have made all the difference in the world.

CONCLUSION

AS I READ MY MANUSCRIPT over many times, it seemed to me there was still something missing. After spending so many long hours in the company of my memories, taking great care in selecting the right words to express the appropriate emotion. After meticulously weaving each picture, and each borrowed quote, to see if they truly expressed what I was trying to say. After revising, meditating, praying. After submitting my ideas and texts to the expertise of good friends and writers. After adding the necessary corrections here and there and taking out the superfluous. After thoroughly screening my motives to make sure that my goal wasn't to draw attention to myself or to inspire pity. After coming back time and time again to the sketch Micah left me, listening to hear clearly what he wanted to tell me. After surrendering to all three characters so they could peer inside me and reveal all that was there. After all my attempts to bring, through my book, a ray of light to those who face only darkness. After offering my friendship to those who are tortured by remorse or crushed by discouragement. After putting down my pen and storing away the ink bottle... I had to sincerely admit that something was still missing!

What I searched for in my memories, what I tried to express on paper, what I tried to hear from the notes of each song, what the sea didn't tell me, what I did not read in the verses of the poems nor in any sentence of my work — this something that is missing, this someone, I know, is Micah.

Nothing and no one will ever be able to replace him. My heart will always ache at his absence, although the eyes of my soul already peer into eternity and imagine the moment when I will see him again.

I end here, expressing my complete gratitude to my best friend, my confidante and my Saviour, the Lord Jesus Christ. His love endured and never failed, even in the worst moments of my deepest agony. He is the Resurrection and the Life, and

I know that one day I will see him, with my beautiful Micah, and together we will be united for eternity.

The true Light that gives light to every man was coming into the world. He was in the world, and though the world was made through him, the world did not recognize him.

He came to that which was his own, but his own did not receive him. Yet to all who received him, to those who believed in his name, he gave the right to become children of God.

(GOSPEL OF JOHN, CHAPTER 1)

EPILOGUE

I WOULD NOT WANT to end without offering you the opportunity to receive the love and forgiveness of God. There is no mountain so high, nor valley so deep that God cannot reach. There is no mistake so serious that God cannot forgive. All that is needed is to ask him. Praying is a step in the right direction. I encourage you to read the following prayer as if spoken from your own heart. God promised he would welcome all that come to him with a sincere heart.

"Lord Jesus, I acknowledge my need of you. I thank you for coming to earth because of your love for me, and for dying on the cross to free me from condemnation and sin. I ask you to forgive me for all of the wrongs I have done, for the little sins as well as the more serious ones. I ask you to wash my conscience clean and help me to forgive myself, and others, just as you forgive me.

I invite you to live in my heart and be my best friend. Please take my hand in yours and guide me step by step, every day of my life.

I want to be yours and love you forever."

RESOURCES

Help Centers for Youth in Crisis

Telephone numbers for Help Centers for Youth in Crisis in your area are listed in the front pages of your city phonebook. These help lines usually operate 24 hours a day, 7 days a week.

In some cases help lines are strictly for the youth and only for a certain number of hours per day. Help lines for people in crisis can be very busy and you may have to wait a while, or phone again a number of times before eventually reaching someone. Don't give up; keep trying.

If you live far from the Help Center for your area and have to pay for long distance, dial "0" and tell the operator you're trying to reach a help line. The operator may be able to transfer you directly without charge. Some of the centers have toll-free numbers that cover a large territory.

An Adult You Can Trust

This could be someone who has gained your trust in the past, or someone you know would care about you and be eager to find help for you. Take care, however! Not everyone is trustworthy, regardless of their profession. Make sure you feel safe with them. Choose one of two people you can trust and find a way to talk to them. This person could be any of the following:

- Your parents
- The mother or father of a friend
- An aunt, uncle or other member of your family

- A classmate from school (they may not be an
  adult, but often they may know what to do to help)
- A priest, a pastor or a counsellor at your church
- A youth supervisor in a club you belong to
- A counsellor at your school
- A psychologist
- A doctor, nurse, or other healthcare worker

**Les Éditions Jaspe is a non-profit organization.
All proceeds from the sale of this book will be
used to fund suicide prevention.**

LES ÉDITIONS JASPE
C.P. 801
MAGOG (QUEBEC)
J1X 5C6
www.jaspe.org